WHOLEIFY
your dog

LISA ST. JOHN

ARTEMIS

&

AURORA

Publishing

54th West 40th St

New York, NY 10018

Copyright © 2020 by Lisa St. John

All rights reserved. No part of this publication may be reproduced, stored in a retrieval system, or transmitted in any form or by any means – electronic, mechanical, photocopy, recording, or any other – except for brief quotations in printed reviews or articles, without the prior written permission of the publisher.

Second edition 2020.

Proudly printed in the United States of America.

"A dog is the only thing on earth that loves you more than he loves himself."

JOSH BILLINGS

This book is dedicated to my clients - helping your animals regain health and vitality through the power of nature has been my great honor. I am forever grateful to you and your animals for the many years of learning and growing and being a part of this amazing journey.

I also want to thank Julie Guest – my client, friend and marketing consultant. Without this amazing lady this book would not be possible. Thank you for all your help, support, respect and dedication in helping my message reach so many people.

I also want to thank Nancy and Bob Craigmyle who have always believed in me and my dreams.

I want to thank my own beloved dogs and horses for the lessons they have taught me and their unconditional support and love through the years.

And finally, I dedicate this book to you – the reader, for having the curiosity and determination to find a better path to health for your own animals.

Here's to upleveling the health of all our animals everywhere!

CONTENTS

	Introduction	**1**
1.	Canis Lupus Familiaris – Understanding the Dog Species	**5**
2.	Why So Much Disease in Our Dogs?	**19**
	- Understanding the Chemistry of Health and Disease	**21**
3.	Cleaning out the "Sewage System"	**27**
	- Understanding (and Celebrating) the Detoxification Process	**29**
4.	Good Herbs, "Bad Herbs" and Why the Right Herbs are so Important to Treat the Body and Support the Healing Process	**33**
	- History and Background of Herbal Medicine	**33**
	- The Unique Healing Power of Herbs	**35**
5.	Iridology – A Powerful Diagnostic Tool for Determining the True State of your Dog's Health	**39**
	- Understanding The Four Stages Of Illness As Reflected In The Iris	**40**
	- Treating the Body not Illness	**41**
6.	Transitioning Your Dog to the WHOLEify Way of Eating	**45**
	- List of Natural Foods for your Dog	**46**
	- Transition Menu	**47**
	- Key Ingredients that are a "Must Have" Daily.	**51**

	- Recommended Product: Immune Enhancer	**52**
	- Changes you will Notice while your Dog is on a Natural Raw Food Diet	**53**
7.	Healing Food & Delicious Homemade Treat Recipes	**55**
8.	Natural Remedies and First Aid	**63**
	- Natural Remedies	**63**
	- Injuries & First Aid	**67**
	- Natural Remedies for Common Ailments	**73**
9.	WHOLEify Your Puppy	**77**
Conclusion		**87**
Client Stories		**89**
Take The #WHOLEify 30 Day Challenge		**97**
Promo Code #HeartMyDog		**101**
About Lisa St. John		**103**
References		**107**

Introduction

Welcome to a brand new way of looking at your dog's health and a step-by-step Wellness Guide to ensure your dog lives a long, healthy life.

Whatever the reason you picked up this book, it is not by chance you are here. We are facing a health crisis of epidemic proportions that is affecting both people, as well as their pets.

More people are dying from cancer than has ever been recorded in history. Between 2010 - 2019 the American Cancer Society projected that the number of new cancer cases in the USA would rise by 22%. Nearly two million people were diagnosed with cancer last year in the USA. That's in addition to the 15.5 million people living with cancer.

Unfortunately this trend runs parallel with our animals also.

Fifty years ago one in every 100 dogs got cancer. Today the Animal Cancer Society reports that over 6 million dogs are diagnosed with cancer every year. Dr. Martin Goldstein, a DVM with over 45 years experience recently made this observation: "When I graduated from Cornell in 1973, approximately one out of 10 dogs got cancer and it was always a disease of the "old". So if we saw a dog that had a lump and the dog was young, we eliminated cancer as a possibility, just based on age. We do now see – commonly - dogs under 18 months of age with terminal cancer, and what used to be a disease of the old is now, unfortunately a disease of the young."

These statistics are horrifying. They are enough to make any of us heart broken in advance of adopting a new dog. **But the good news is that it does not have to be this way.** No matter whether you are reading this book with a chronically sick dog at home, or if you've just opened your heart to adopt a brand new family member, **once you understand what is causing the disease in our dogs, treating the body and preventing disease becomes simple.**

A word of warning however.

If you are someone who is stuck in a traditional allopathic mindset, have difficulty following instructions, or are looking for an overnight magic pill – then this book is not for you. Please return it to where you purchased it from and ask for your money back. I have spent close to 25 years developing, testing and implementing wellness programs for thousands of dogs and horses all over the world. I know what works and the results speak for themselves.

This program WILL work for your dog. It doesn't matter if you have a 3 pound teacup poodle or a 200 pound Irish Wolf Hound. It doesn't matter whether your dog is a pampered pooch or a working farm dog. WHOLEify works for all dogs, all ages, all stages. Period.

It was the great Greek philosopher, Hippocrates, who once said,
"The natural forces within us are the true healers of disease."

This book is about treating the body, the most magnificent and complex machine ever created, which surprisingly we know so little about.

I'm so glad you're here. Let's get started on your dog's journey to full health.

Lisa St John

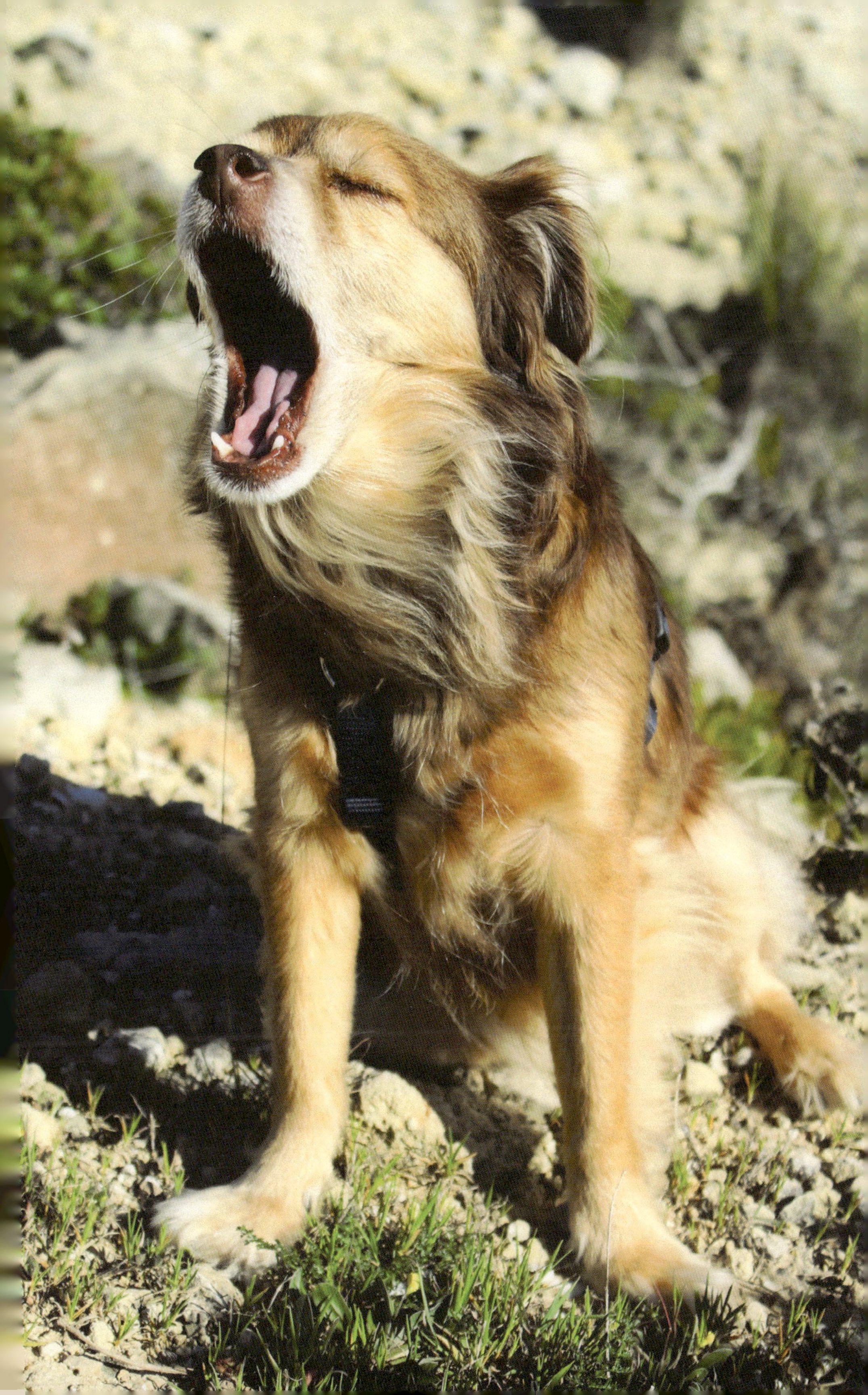

"THE WORLD WOULD BE A NICER PLACE IF EVERYONE HAD THE ABILITY TO LOVE AS UNCONDITIONALLY AS A DOG."

— MK Clinton

Chapter 1
Canis Lupus Familiaris - Understanding the Dog Species

"Dogs feel very strongly that they should always go with you in the car, in case the need should arise for them to bark violently at nothing right in your ear."

DAVE BARRY

When Rover is lovingly sitting at your feet, carrying your favorite pair of slippers around in his mouth , chasing a tennis ball, or playing tug-of-war with a brand new cashmere sweater, it can be easy to forget that our beautiful family member is a direct descendant of the noble wolf!

The Friendly Wolf Dog

Genetic scientific researchers have proven that dogs are genetically linked to the wolf. The scientific name for the dog, or domestic canine, is Canis lupus familiaris. This scientific name is of Latin origin, and the literal meaning is "friendly wolf dog."

In 1993, there was a reclassification of the scientific name for domestic dogs. Prior to this time, its scientific classification was Canis familiaris and Canis familiaris domesticus. While Canis was the genus, familiaris domesticus was the species. Carolus Linnaeus gave the dog these assignations in 1758.

However, in 1993, these classifications were reassigned to its present scientific name by the Smithsonian Institution and the American Association of Mammalogists. This scientific name includes the fact that domesticated dog breeds descends from wolves, and have been linked to a 30,000 year old wolf fossil. This genetic link is much closer to that of the modern day gray wolf. Science has proven that dogs derive from a European species of wolf during the Ice Age, 30,000 years ago.

The oldest signs of domestication in wolf came from Goyet Cave in Belgium. This wolf was a short- skulled wolf dating back 31,700 years.

Genetic Scientists have determined that wolves and dogs share 99.9% of their DNA confirming they are in fact the same species, this species being canine.

What Wolves & Dogs Eat

Canines are omnivores. This is scientifically proven by their own anatomical and physiological makeup. So, what exactly is an omnivore? I'm so glad you asked! An omnivore is a kind of animal that eats animal protein and plants. Some omnivores will hunt and eat their food, like carnivores, who eat herbivores. Some omnivores are scavengers and will eat dead matter as well as eggs.

Omnivores Diet

Omnivores eat plants, but not *all* kinds of plants. Unlike the herbivore, omnivores can't digest some of the substances in grains or other plants that do not produce fruit. They can, however, eat fruits and vegetables.

Omnivores are biologically suited to consume vegetation, herbs, vegetables, fruits, nuts, seeds, roots, some barks, meat protein, and bone. Notice that omnivores are not suited to eat grains.

When I mention tree bark that always raises an eye brow! Haven't you ever seen a dog chewing on a stick? That's for good reason. This is actually part of their natural diet. Why would dogs need tree bark? Because many tree barks contain medicinal properties. White oak bark for example is anti-parasitic, anti-fungal, and anti-bacterial. It is also a digestive tonic and settles and soothes an upset stomach. White Willow bark is an anti-inflammatory and is used in aspirin. Tree barks have been used to treat a wide range of ailments from inflammation through to arthritis, and high blood pressure. Your dog instinctively knows what its body needs – if they grab a stick and start chewing on it – let them chew it! They know what their body needs!

The body is a complete unit of inner workings made up of chemistry and energy making up its own unique terrain. The terrain is what influences health.

Racing grey hounds and sled dogs have long eaten raw food diets. Extending those feeding practices to the family pet is a more recent idea, that was officially proposed in 1993 by Australian veterinarian, Ian Billinghurst.

Dr. Bilinghurst has worked in companion animal practice since 1975. In the mid 1980s following years of clinical research he was shocked to realize the devastating effect that commercial foods had on dog and cat health and was amazed at the dramatic healing power of raw. He called his feeding suggestions the BARF diet, an acronym that stands for Bones and Raw Food, or Biologically Appropriate Raw Food.

Dr. Billinghurst's research showed that adult dogs thrived on an evolutionary diet based on what canines ate before they became domesticated. Raw, meaty bones and vegetables. *Grain based commercial pet foods, he contended, were harmful to a dog's health.*

Commercial Pet Foods

Let's dig into this issue of commercial pet foods a little deeper. Commercial pet food has not been around very long – and before that humans were feeding their dogs meat, vegetables, fruit, table scraps. Whole, unprocessed food.

So why did we all of a sudden switch to commercial grade food and, most importantly why do so few people understand the real ingredients? Even with the "organic and natural" ingredients, commercial pet food is on the bottom rung of the nutritional ladder. For as long as most of us can remember, pet food has always arrived in a bag. But before dogs became domesticated, in the mid-1800s, dogs primarily lived outside and ate raw meat or table scraps. It was only after the Industrial Revolution with the growth of a more affluent middle class which led to cats and dogs becoming house pets who were considered more "civilized" companions than their outdoor, working counterparts.

Let's examine the history of commercial pet food which has only been around for 150 years (compare that to dogs which have been recorded as far back as 36,500 years ago).

It All Began With Flour, Water & Salt – Yum! Dry Biscuits!

The world's first commercial pet food was developed in 1860 by an electrician from Cincinnatti called James Spratt. After traveling from Ohio to the United Kingdom to sell lightning rods, James noticed dogs along the riverbanks in Northern London were eating leftover "hardtack" – the dry biscuit sailors ate on long trips.

Made of flour, water, and occasionally salt, these crackers were very cheap to produce and lasted for months without refrigeration. Mr. Spratt concluded that dog owners were also in need of a shelf-stable food option for their pets, so he set about creating the world's first dog biscuit which he promoted as a complete meal.

Called "Spratt's Meat Fibrine Dog Cakes," the dog biscuits contained a mix of blended wheat, vegetables, beetroot, and "the dried unsalted gelatinous parts of Prairie Beef". (Interestingly but not surprisingly James Spratt refused to disclose his biscuits' specific meat source during his lifetime). The biscuits were expensive to produce and were sold as a luxury item for dogs with one 50 pound bag costing the equivalent of an entire day's work for a skilled craftsman!

After launching the company's American operations in the 1870s, James Spratt began advertising en masse. He began targeting health conscious pet owners and dog show participants and purchased the front cover of the first American Kennel Club journal in January 1889.

To help him promote his product, Mr Spratt used testimonials from wealthy, English country gentlemen. They sang the praises of Spratt's dog cakes. The American public was hooked. Very quickly people stopped feeding their dogs table scraps and meat and replaced their meals with Spratt's dog biscuits instead.

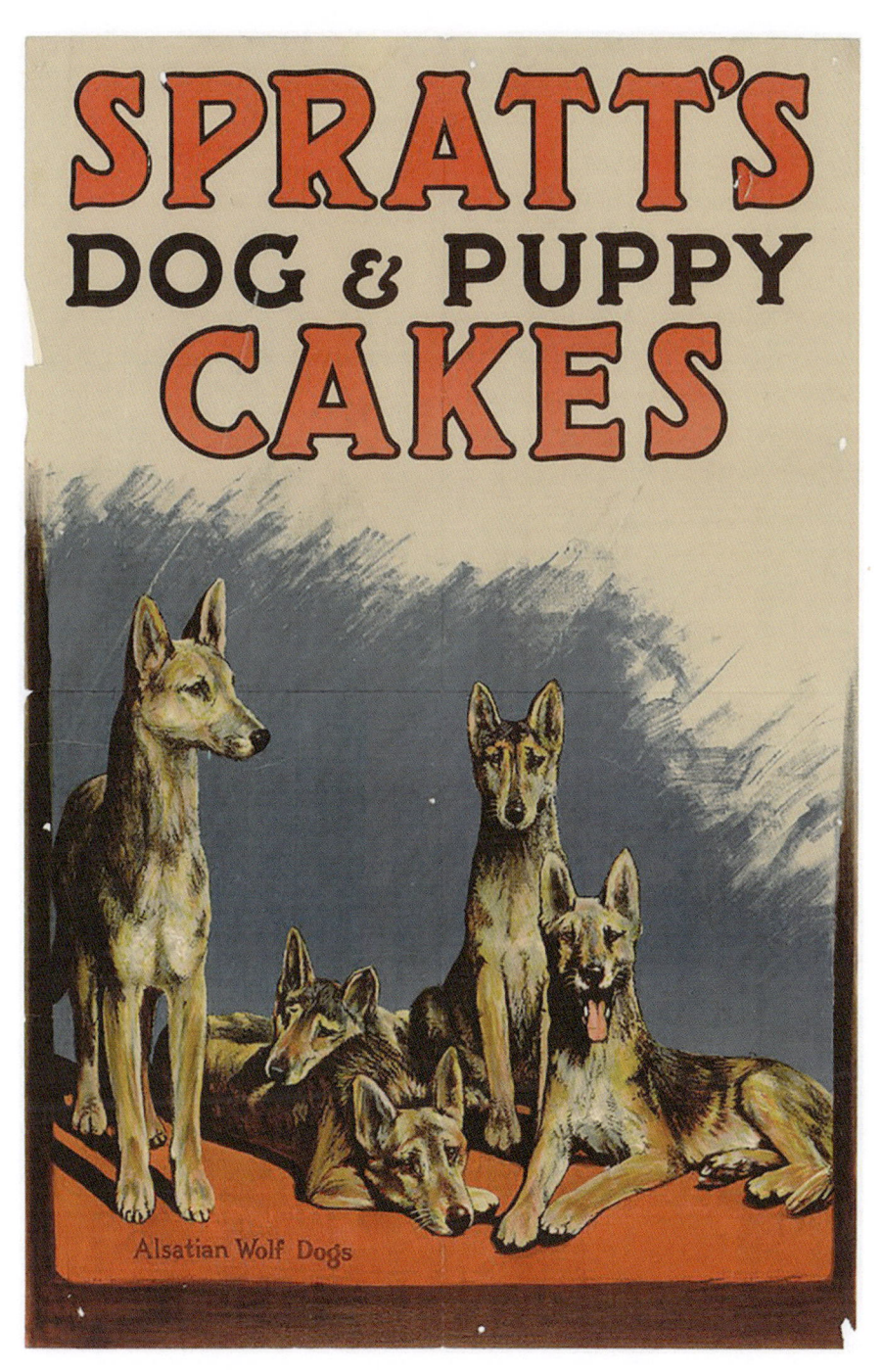

Canis Lupus Familiaris - Understanding the Dog Species

1900s: Mass Adoption Continues

By the early 1900s, more people were taking notice of the commercial pet food market.

In 1907, the F.H. Bennett Company in New York City began making Milk Bone™ dog biscuits. Ken-L Ration® introduced canned horse meat for dogs after World War I, and Gaines Food® introduced canned cat food and dry meat-meal dog food in the 1930s. The pet food race was on.

By 1941, canned food was such a commercial success that manufacturers were breeding horses just for dog food and slaughtering 50,000 of them per year.

But when tin and meat were rationed during World War II and pet food was classified as a "non-essential" item, pet food manufacturers had to get creative. The combination of these imposed rations combined with outrage from animal lovers who were furious about the number of horses being killed every year for dog food, led to the creation of a new pet food "innovation" in 1956 – a process called extrusion that produced the first dry kibble.

Extrusion is a method used for manufacturing large quantities of shelf-stable foods (for example breakfast cereals). Wet and dry ingredients are mixed together to form a dough-like consistency, and then fed into a machine called an expander. The dough is cooked under pressurized steam and high temperatures before being extruded (or pushed) through a die cut machine to form it into the small shapes – the kibble.

The use of extrusion for commercial kibble production gained momentum throughout the 1960s and 1970s as companies used the technology to create new flavors, shapes and varieties. The foods must contain large amounts of starch for the extrusion process to work.

Nutrients are added back in to make up for the nutrient loss, due to the double cooking process at high temperatures. Fats and flavorings are then sprayed on the end product to make them more palatable.[7]

In the 1950s and 60s, many food companies began to add pet foods products to their line. For example companies such as General Foods®, Quaker Oats®, Campbell's® Soups, Mars®, Lipton®, Post®, Carnation® and Nabisco® started manufacturing pet foods and *saw them as a profitable way to market their by-products.*[4]

Companies began marketing their pet food products as "complete foods", and started the idea that feeding our animals table scraps was actually dangerous. In 1964, The Pet Food Institute launched a campaign warning consumers about the dangers of feeding table scraps and the importance of feeding kibble to pets to persuade consumers that commercial dog food was the only healthy option! The campaigns were successful.

Once kibble had been established as the leading pet food, advertising strategies became more sophisticated. The marketing of "prescription" pet foods began sold primarily through veterinarians. This was initially done by Hill's® (which was purchased by Colgate Palmolive® in 1976) after their parent company had success marketing toothpastes through dentists.[9]

2000s – Today: QUESTION EVERYTHING

Today, pet food companies still produce kibble using extrusion because it facilitates flexibility and density control and better pasteurization, and extends the shelf life. But here's the rub: why do all the pet food ads show fresh fruit and vegetables and real beef, chicken, lamb or fish as their key ingredients? *If this is the case then why don't we just feed our dogs real fruit and vegetables and real meat?*

Another key part of the message in pet food marketing was that pet food is complicated and best left to the "professionals" as they were the only ones who knew what pets really needed to eat.

Dr. Judy Morgan "What you're taught in school is never let your clients do a home-cooked meal. Do not feed them anything from the table. Oh my gosh, God forbid if they feed scraps from the table they will unbalance a balanced diet that they're pouring with the kibble into the bowl...what a bunch of malarkey."

Dr. Rick Pamquist "When I was in veterinary school, we were taught. 'Don't put anything in the dog food. Feed a complete and balanced dog food designed by nutritionists and companies. We have good control over what's going into these things. And if you add other foods, you mess up the nutritional balance of the food.'

But we know that chronic inflammation is the root of all chronic disease. And so, if we're feeding a food that causes chronic inflammation, we've got to do something about it. Otherwise we're just the kind of unethical car salesmen; we're cashing - in on sick dogs."

Dr. Karen Becker "When it comes to nutrition, there're a lot of issues in the pet food industry we are up against... and I believe that how we choose to nourish our animals on a day-to-day basis absolutely impacts their immunologic health. So there again veterinarians will tell you never switch your pet's food. We're supposed to wean your puppy, let's say at 5 weeks of age. You put them on an entirely inorganic, over-processed, dehydrated, 'nutritionally complete and balanced' dead food. I want you to think of it like Total – we're not picking on Total cereal. But think of it like Total cereal. So you take a regular cereal. You add a synthetic multivitamin to it. Would you feed that to your kid three times a day? Probably not...Veterinarians have convinced an entire 100 years of pet owners that if you fed anything other than pet food, dry kibble, or canned food, you could be harming your pet. In fact, veterinarians are the only wellness professionals that actually tell you to eat more processed foods, and fresh food is risky... in vet school we are not taught nutrition matters."

Dr. Judy Morgan "I can only think that that got started from the big, pet food companies who said, 'Well, we're going to teach veterinarians, who are then going to teach their clients, for the patients. And then all of our commercials on TV say you must feed them this 100% complete and balanced diet in their bowl every single day…and so actually I got a box of cereal, and we made a new cover for it, and we put on the front "Human Kibble". And it says on there 100% complete and nutritionally balanced." And then it's got its vitamin list on the back and all the ingredients.'

And I say to people all the time,

'Okay here's your human kibble. I'm going to pour this in your bowl twice a day. You don't get milk, nothing on it. I'm going to pour this dry cereal in your bowl and this is what you get to eat, twice a day for the rest of your life…how are we feeling? Feeling good about that? I'm thinking you're going to have some big deficiencies because adding a synthetic chemical/vitamin/mineral mix is not the same as getting whole food nutrition from real plants, real meat. It's not feeding the species-appropriate diet….'

Our dogs and cats are not out there foraging for synthetic chemicals. My cats go outside. They bring me back bunnies and mice and moles. They're getting a species-appropriate diet. They're pretty dang healthy."

Dr. Elizabeth Pantzer "I have a masters degree in dairy nutrition and I can't read the labels on pet food. The pet food industry uses terms that have no meaning, especially related to our commonly accepted meanings. So "natural" means nothing in human or pet food labeling. Chicken meal does not mean what we think it means on the labeling…we need an unabridged dictionary.. to go through to be able to read the labels, like a thesaurus where we can work out, 'I think this word means this', and then you look it up and you say,

'Oh no this is what the word means in the industry.'"

Dr. Gary Richter: "Where I went to school there was a lot of funding provided by pet food companies. Just as an example: as a veterinary student, everybody in my class and every student in the veterinary school got a free bag of dog food from two different pet food companies every month. They did a really excellent job at buying brand loyalty at a very early age. And what the practical result of that is, is that most veterinarians, take a very over-simplified approach to nutrition."

Dr. Laurin Cooke: "As vet students, we were all given free food from Science Diet from Hills. That was part of the program. So our nutrition exposure was pretty limited to critical care nutrition, - in your medicine rounds for the really sick animals and trying to figure out how to feed them with feeding tubes, that kind of thing… and then there was the food we were getting from Hills for our own animals. And there wasn't much of anything about real nutrition. And you never really questioned it because yeah, it's Science Diet. It's supposed to be better than the stuff you get at the grocery store, right? And so that's what we'd sell and there would be a prescription diet for every problem and it comes in a bag and it's easy so you don't have to think about it."

Dr. Allen Schoen: "When I was in veterinary school, I was excited. I had no money. I borrowed, I had scholarships, I worked part-time. I did everything I could to survive. And I was elated that they were giving me free dog food. And in our nutrition course back then at Cornell, the nutritionist said, 'You are so busy with all your other courses. Here's all the information from different food companies, and just study that and you'll be fine.' And so, yes, it just didn't feel quite right. But also, you were excited that you got free food when you're trying to make it to get through vet school. When I first got out of vet school, that's what I was feeding…and I thought I was doing a good job.

We're programmed. You can't really blame veterinarians. We're programmed that that's okay. It wasn't until my cat started developing liver disease that I started questioning, "What am I feeding him?".

Regulation Of Pet Food Industry

Pet food manufacturers are regulated at the federal level by the FDA, under the Federal Food, Drug, and Cosmetic Act (FFDCA). Within the FDA, the Center for Veterinary Medicine (CVM) is responsible for the regulation of animal feed products, **although they do not set any standards for pet food,** and only regulate animal drugs, medicated feeds (which are almost entirely for livestock) and food additives. **There is no pre-market approval requirement for pet foods.**[10]

The FDA fulfills its mandate for pet food regulation by partnering with an organization called the Association of American Feed Control Officials (AAFCO), which states it is "an organization almost entirely independent of government control." Unfortunately **AAFCO has no enforcement authority and does not perform any analytical testing on pet food.** A pet food manufacturer is only required to comply with the pet food regulations of the state in which it manufactures or sells its products.[11]

If you're interested in learning more about how commercial pet food is produced, or what really goes into it, then I would encourage you to do a google search. Just be prepared for what you will find.

And thankfully, this discussion brings us full circle back to the Raw Food movement. Feeding our dogs ....like dogs!

The Origins of the Raw Food Movement

The raw food movement for dogs is not new. It's as old as the dog species itself (over 37,000 years). There are plenty of people out there who have been raw feeding their dogs – and cats – successfully for decades. There are a growing number of small companies, frequently small natural or organic farmers working on a local level, that are filling the demand by pet owners for a healthier and more natural way to feed their animals.

Take our #WHOLEify30DayChallenge at the back of this book and see the visible results for yourself- you will be astounded! We would love to see your results – please email us a "before" phone and an "after" photo to hello@WHOLEify.com

However transitioning your dog to a raw food, species specific diet is just the first step in restoring their health.

As you will see in an upcoming chapter, correctly sourced and formulated herbs play a critical role in recovery and long-term health so get ready to read on!

But first a quick recap on why the first step to "wholeness" for your dog must be to feed them a species specific raw diet:

Steps To Wholeness — Why A Species Specific Raw Diet?

1. Boosts and helps heal and repair the immune system.
2. Alkalizes the body (we want an alkaline body and NOT an acidic one which is where disease thrives).
3. Promotes a shiny, healthy coat that is softer and smoother. Some of our clients report their dog's new coat feels "as soft as velvet."
4. Eliminates dog odor.
5. Eliminates bad breath.
6. Eliminates flatulence.
7. Promotes healthy gums.
8. Provides whiter/healthier teeth - tarter chips away due to the alkalinity in the saliva. It is acid that creates tarter - alkalinity neutralizes acids.
9. Increases focus and concentration - trainability and mindful awareness is sharpened.
10. Increased mobility and fluidity of motion.
11. Relieves joint pain.
12. Eyes become clear and less foggy.
13. Prevents and aids in recovery of allergies and hot spots.

14. Much lower parasites and fungus counts - due to providing an alkaline environment in which they cannot thrive.
15. Dogs who have been on a raw diet for 6+ months have biodegradable stools. They will turn white and blow away, resulting in a self-sustainable yard cleanup - nature takes care of it.
16. Dogs will consume less water as a result of being hydrated on a cellular level through alkaline forming foods. Alkaline pH = hydration Acid pH = Dehydration
17. Prevents degenerative and chronic conditions by providing an environment (alkaline pH) in which disease and illness cannot thrive.
18. Dogs will be recognized for their species and will NOT be mistaken as a prey mammal. Note: only carnivores and omnivores consume animal protein. Lions, wolves, coyotes, mountain lions/cougars, prey on herbivores, (grass eating mammals) not meat eaters. Think of the animals in Africa - Clawed mammals (carnivores/omnivores) prey on hoofed mammals (herbivores). A clawed mammal never attacks another clawed mammal for food consumption, they will only fight for territory. On a species friendly raw diet your dog will carry an omnivore scent . This will naturally ward off any predators looking for their next meal.

These are just a few positive changes and benefits to feeding a species friendly diet. But don't take my word for it.

Take our 30-day Challenge at the back of this book and see the visible results for yourself – you will be astounded.

Now let's move into the heart of this book – understanding the chemistry of what is causing the disease in our dogs, and how to treat the body not the illness allowing the body to regain health and vitality so your dog can live a long, healthy life.

"DOGS LAUGH, BUT THEY LAUGH WITH THEIR TAILS."

Chapter 2
Why So Much Disease In Our Dogs?

"My little dog—a heartbeat at my feet."

EDITH WHARTON

According to the American Veterinary Medical Association, the 3 leading causes of death in our dogs are:

1. Cancer
2. Kidney Failure
3. Diabetes

Dogs Have The Highest Rate Of Cancer Of Any Mammal On The Planet

Fifty years ago 1 in every 100 dogs got cancer. Today the Animal Cancer Society reports that over 6 million dogs are diagnosed with cancer every year.

In one year, the cancer rate in dogs jumped from 1 in 2 dogs to 1 in every 1.65 dogs.

These statistics are a horrifying reality check.

In the previous chapter you read the quote by Dr. Martin Goldstein who said when he graduated from Cornell University in 1973, approximately 1 out of 10 dogs were diagnosed with cancer and it was always a disease that affected the older dogs. Now dogs under 18 months old are being diagnosed with terminal cancer.

It's time we all take a step back and begin making some major changes to improve the health and wellness of our dogs.

Hundreds of billions of dollars have been spent researching cancer and its causes. The American Institute for Cancer Research concluded that acid forming foods alter the body's pH balance and "promotes cancer". This is based on lab studies that show cancer cells thrive in an acidic environment and cannot thrive in an alkaline (base) environment.

Studies have suggested that acidic pH increases the ability for cancer to spread. A team of Swedish scientists developed a new cancer cell line that grew under acidic conditions. They developed this cell line by continuously growing this cancer strand by placing a batch of human colon cells in a specialized broth containing an acid pH for over three months.

It is no secret to the medical community that cancer thrives in an acid terrain.

Yet still, with the understanding that cancer is caused by acids, the allopathic professionals choose to use an acid based chemical treatment (chemotherapy) to treat cancer. Which explains why the medical community has yet to find a cure for cancer.

Here are some quotes from Veterinarians and Doctors who were interviewed in the documentary, *"The Truth About Pet Cancer"* by Ty Bollinger.

Dr. Alexandra Niedzwiecki

"Chemotherapy uses the most powerful toxins known to humans, and these toxins of course, are being sold to us as substances that can kill cancer cells. But these substances also kill and annihilate healthy cells in the body, damage organs, which makes recovery from cancer almost a miracle or impossible. The very chemicals they use to fight cancer are cancer causing.

One of the reasons why this war continues is the money that is being made in this war. And this refers to the treatments, so called 'treatments', that are being used in cancer, namely chemotherapy."

Dr. Peter Dobias

"I think the problem with these treatments is that instead of supporting and enhancing the body's own immunity and defense, we end up poisoning the body. It's like pouring sewage in a lake and thinking that we are going to purify it by pouring sewage in it.

"It is sad to know that doctors, the healers, are the third leading cause of death in the United States. We worry about sharks, we worry about flying on planes. While ironically, and this is hard to say because I am a doctor, doctors are more 'dangerous' than any of these causes. We don't intend to harm, but we have been taught a system that doesn't work."

Dr. Mathew Rath

"In order to have maximum chance of fighting and overcoming cancer, we need an intact immune system, and that too, makes the current approach to chemotherapy so unethical."

Dr. Martin Goldstein

"If we have to use something that is known to cause cancer – radiation is immune suppressive and causes cancer – to treat cancer – we have failed in the field of healthcare. Period."

* **Allopathic or allopathy** refers to science based, modern medicine, such as the use of medications or surgery to treat or suppress symptoms or the ill effects of disease.

Understanding The Chemistry Of Health And Disease

Chemistry plays an important role in the anatomy and physiology of your dog. There are two sides to chemistry – alkaline (base) and acid.

In nature everything is connected, which brings about a natural system of balance. The ability to achieve that balance, requires two opposing sides;

hot and cold, negative and positive, big and small, electron and neutron, night and day, acid and alkaline. When there is a duality – or opposites, there is the ability to achieve that perfect balance.

A pH scale is used to rank the relative alkaline (base) or acid of substances based on the amount of hydrogen ion activity - pH stands for (Potential Hydrogen). This scale is 0-14. **The lower the pH, the more acidic the solution is.** The perfectly balanced pH for your dog is 7.0-7.3.

Everything is made up of chemistry and physics (energy), including your dog's body. The body's biological environment is measured by the pH scale.

- Alkaline (base) side of chemistry is the cooling side of chemistry. Alkaline heals, repairs, nurtures, creates. It is the creative healing side of chemistry.
- Acid side of chemistry is just like it sounds - Acid is hot, burns, destroys, tears apart. Acid is the corrosive side of chemistry.

Too much of one thing is never good. Being over alkaline is just as harmful as being over acidic. However, it is much more difficult to become over alkaline. The very air we breath affects the pH in the body which is why I treat animals in different parts of the world very differently. Equally I would not prescribe the same blend of herbs to treat a dog suffering from bone cancer in Florida, the same as a dog with bone cancer in Minnesota. Both dogs live in completely different environments which affect their pH balance dramatically.

Maintaining that perfect pH can only be achieved by what we have control over - such as what we eat, drink, put on our skin, what remedies we use, cleaning supplies, and even the laundry detergent we use to wash our dogs beds, blankets and those little adorable doggie jackets.

This duality of acid and alkaline makes it very easy to create a balance which is needed to create a harmonious environment within the body's terrain.

Harmful bacteria, parasites, and fungi all thrive in an acid environment. Disease, illness, viruses, and chronic degenerative conditions are also born in an acid terrain.

Acid mutates and damages cells.

How does a cell become mutated and damaged? The body is chemistry – there are only two sides. Which side do you think would mutate, damage and corrode a cell? The acid side of course. A cancer cell isn't a cell that flew in from outer-space to attack the body. Everything is cause and effect. The effect of a mutated "cancer cell" is caused by acids or to be more specific acidic, cellular waste. These cells have been bathing in acidic cellular waste much like the colon cells that the Swedish scientists bathed in the specialized acidic pH broth solution for three months that resulted in their very own home-grown cancer cell strand.

How the body becomes over acidic is achieved in various ways from what one eats, drinks, breaths, puts on their skin as well as stress levels.

When you take your sick dog to the emergency veterinarian hospital or you yourself go to the emergency room the first thing the vet and doctors do is provide an IV of saline solution. Why is this the very first thing they do? Saline solution is a highly alkaline solution. By introducing alkaline chemistry into an acidic medium, it will neutralize the acids achieving a temporary balance, which results in "stabilizing the patient."

The real question is, 'How do we maintain an alkaline pH after the saline solution wears off?"

If we can stabilize the body by injecting an alkaline base solution into the body itself then it would make perfect sense that what one eats, and drinks also effects the pH balance. Consumption is consumption whether it is through an IV or being ingested.

By feeding the body alkaline forming foods introduces alkaline chemistry into the system to stabilize the terrain consistently for a long-term solution. Alkaline forming foods promote a healthy pH balance, providing an environment in which disease, illness, viruses and harmful bacteria cannot thrive. The best offence is defense.

There are trillions of cells that make up every part of your dog's body from hair, fur, organs glands, to bones. They are all comprised of a collection of cells.

These cells are like little people, and like people they need to eat. Consuming foods that are compatible to the species are naturally alkaline forming foods which feed and nourish your dog's cells. Your dog's cells are nourished by the blood. The blood is the kitchen of the body. It brings all the nutrients and nourishment to the cells.

Everything that eats must eliminate. Almost everything has a consumption and an elimination process. In most cases it is the consumption of an alkaline base chemistry and the elimination of an acid base chemistry.

Cellular elimination results in cellular acidic waste.

The body is made up of cells and 2 major fluids. Those 2 fluids are blood and lymphatic fluid.

The blood feeds the cells and the lymphatic system cleanses the cells.

1. The blood is 20% of the body's fluid.
2. The lymphatic system is 80% of the body's fluid.

These two fluids are interstitial fluids which means they flow and move to reach each individual cell in the body and are solely responsible for feeding and cleaning those cells.

The blood is the kitchen of the body, it brings all the goodies to body, while the lymphatic system is the major sewer line of the body that carries away all the cellular waste.

The lymphatic system which makes up 80% of the body's fluid is sadly ignored and misunderstood among the allopathic minds. Yet it is the most important system in the body. It is the very system that prevents disease and illness.

Understanding the lymphatic system is the golden key to health and wellness which brings us to our next chapter, aptly called *"Cleaning Out The Sewage System"*.

Hold your noses, let's go!

"FOR ME A HOUSE OR AN APARTMENT BECOMES A HOME WHEN YOU ADD ONE SET OF FOUR LEGS, A HAPPY TAIL, AND THAT INDESCRIBABLE MEASURE OF LOVE THAT WE CALL A DOG."

- Roger Caras

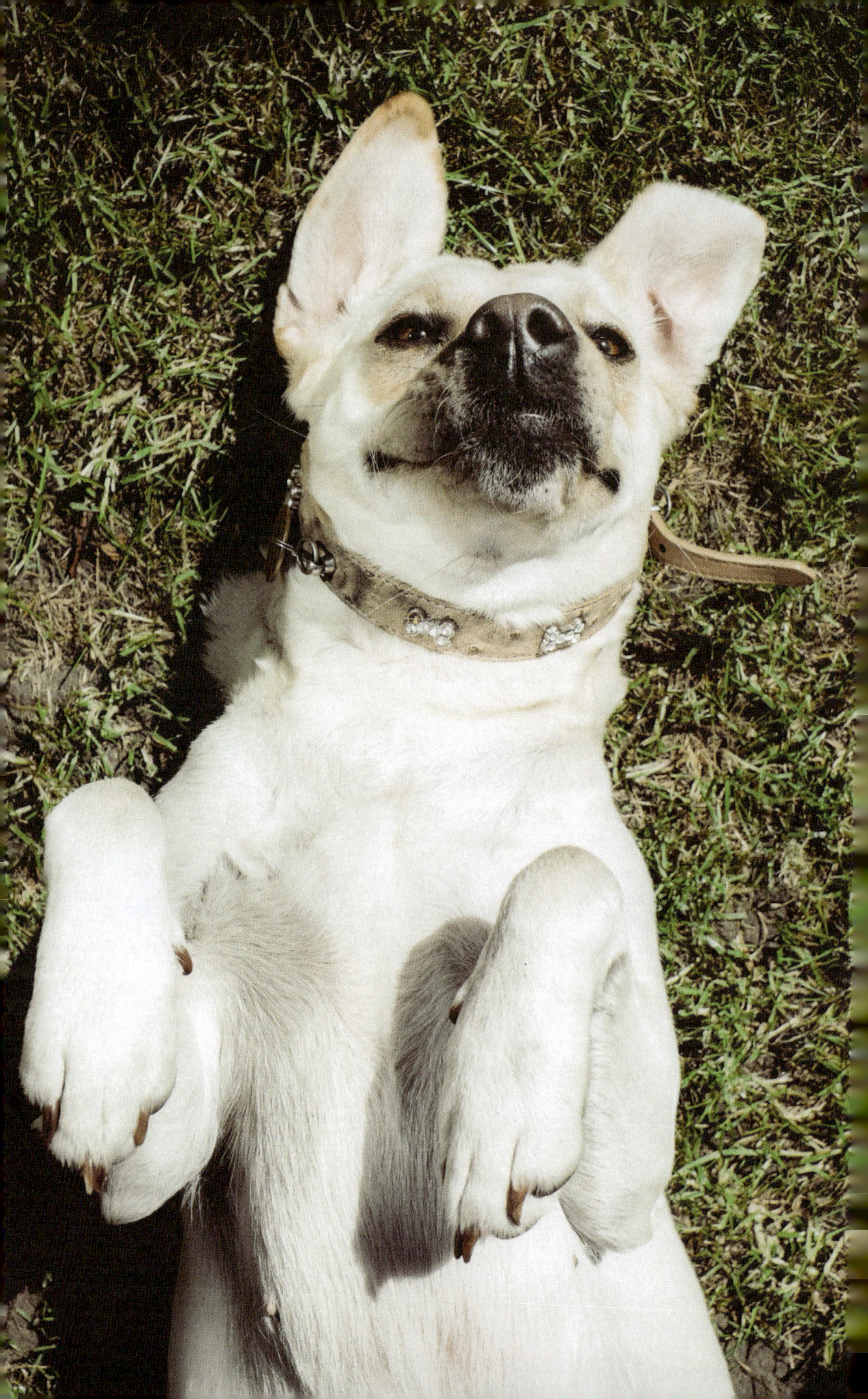

Chapter 3
Cleaning Out The "Sewage System"

"After years of having a dog, you know him. You know the meaning of his snuffs and grunts and barks. Every twitch of the ears is a question or statement, every wag of the tail is an exclamation."

ROBERT MCCAMMON

From reading the last chapter, you now understand the importance of the lymphatic system which makes up over 80% of the body's fluid. Unfortunately the lymphatic system is like the red-headed step child among the allopathic minds – it is sadly misunderstood and largely ignored. Yet it is the most important system in the body. It is the very system that prevents disease and illness. *Let me explain further.*

Your Dog Has 2 Waste Systems: Digestive Waste and Cellular Waste.

- **Digestive waste** travels through the intestines and out the colon.
- **Cellular waste** travels through the lymphatic system which includes the lymph nodes and out the kidneys.

The lymphatic system is a lipid- based system to buffer the acid waste that aids in protecting tissues, vital organs and glands in the body from being damaged during its travels through the body, before it is eliminated out through the kidneys.

The lymph nodes are like the septic tanks in the body. Lymph nodes are cholesterol based to cool down the acid waste as it travels through the body. This cellular waste is hot, it can be as low as 3.0 acid pH which is the pH of vinegar! You do not want your dog urinating at that level, as that would be extremely painful. The lymph nodes (septic tanks) act as cooling tanks. Cholesterol is alkaline based. It will neutralize those acids, so by the time it hits the kidneys, it's somewhere around 6.0 pH, much easier on the kidneys and your dog.

There are lymph nodes throughout your dog's entire system. You may have seen swollen lymph nodes on your dog. Swollen lymph nodes are caused by the inability to eliminate cellular waste properly through the kidneys. If your dog isn't filtering properly this would result in swollen lymph nodes and/or inflammation as well as other symptoms or illnesses. Your dog's urine should never be clear.

Note: If your dog's urine looks like water your dog's kidneys are not filtering properly. There should be "sewage" in the urine which will look yellow or cloudy.

Swollen lymph nodes mean your dog is not filtering properly, resulting in a sluggish lymphatic system (the sewer line is backed up.) Just like your septic tank outside your home if it becomes full, do you remove or empty it? If you remove your septic tank at your house all that sewage backs up in the house. Same thing happens if you remove a lymph node, all of that cellular waste pours directly into the body.

So, what do you do with a swollen lymph node or inflammation? We need to get that sewer line moving which means we need to support those kidneys to get them filtering. We also need to support the adrenal glands which sit on top of the kidneys. Once the kidneys begin to filter, the backed - up cellular waste in the system, including the cellular waste in the swollen lymph node will be able to filter out of the body.

This is called detox.

Understanding (And Celebrating) The Detoxification Process

Detoxification or "detox" for short, is the body's process of removing waste and toxins from the body.

The process of detoxification is probably one of the most misunderstood natural processes in the body. It is an ongoing, VITAL process that the body does (on its own) in order to survive and sustain a healthy terrain by removing toxic waste of every form through the 2 major waste systems: digestive waste system and the lymphatic system.

The majority of the body's fluid (lymphatic system) is designed to eliminate waste – 80% of the lymphatic system's job is to remove cellular waste from the body. Our body was designed to detox.

This detox happens 24/7 365 days of the year.

Almost everyone cringes at the thought of detox. This is due to the fear instilled in us through society to naturally relate to a symptom as an illness, when actually a symptom is nothing more that the body ridding itself of the very cause of what would eventually create the "illness or disease" and that cause would be? All together now – ACIDS.

The allopathic community manages disease or "dis-ease" by treating the symptom. This will only provide the "illusion of health" because they have not addressed the cause.

There is the illusion of health and the reality of health. I prefer the reality of health!

In reality I do not believe in "disease" It's just a question of how toxic is the body? By treating the symptom only, the body is still in an acidic state, which over time will continue to corrode the system. The destruction of cells is what causes illness and disease.

There are four stages of cellular deterioration in the body:

1. Acute
2. Sub-Acute
3. Chronic
4. Degenerative

All of these stages are caused by acidosis. So, in reality call it what you want, cancer, diabetes, allergies, arthritis, or a sore knee, its nothing more than acidosis at different levels and stages, which affect the body.

Remember disease and illness cannot be born in an alkaline environment. But now we have the cellular waste and that needs to be filtered out through the kidneys. The more toxic the system, the more your dog may experience symptoms. I call this "clearings". Clearings are temporary and are by far less painful than the side effects of any chemotherapy treatment.

Each dog will detox differently depending on genetics, and how toxic the body is. The most common detox symptoms are flu like symptoms.

But these clearings are temporary and after each clearing, your dog will be healthier and stronger.

It is inherent in the body to detoxify. To repress a natural function does so much harm. It's so much healthier to support a detox.

Naturopathy treats the body not the illness. For me, as a canine and equine Naturopath, managing health is much more rewarding and works hand in hand with the body's inherent nature to heal itself. There is no cure out there, no magic pill or procedure that will cure anything. Instead the cure is woven in the fabric of our own biological design. The body is the only one that has the ability to heal and repair. All we need to do is support it through Alkaline and Detox.

What supports a detox?

The most powerful and energetic food on the planet. Herbs.

"IN ORDER TO KEEP A TRUE PERSPECTIVE OF ONE'S IMPORTANCE, EVERYONE SHOULD HAVE A DOG THAT WILL WORSHIP HIM AND A CAT THAT WILL IGNORE HIM."

- Derek Bruce

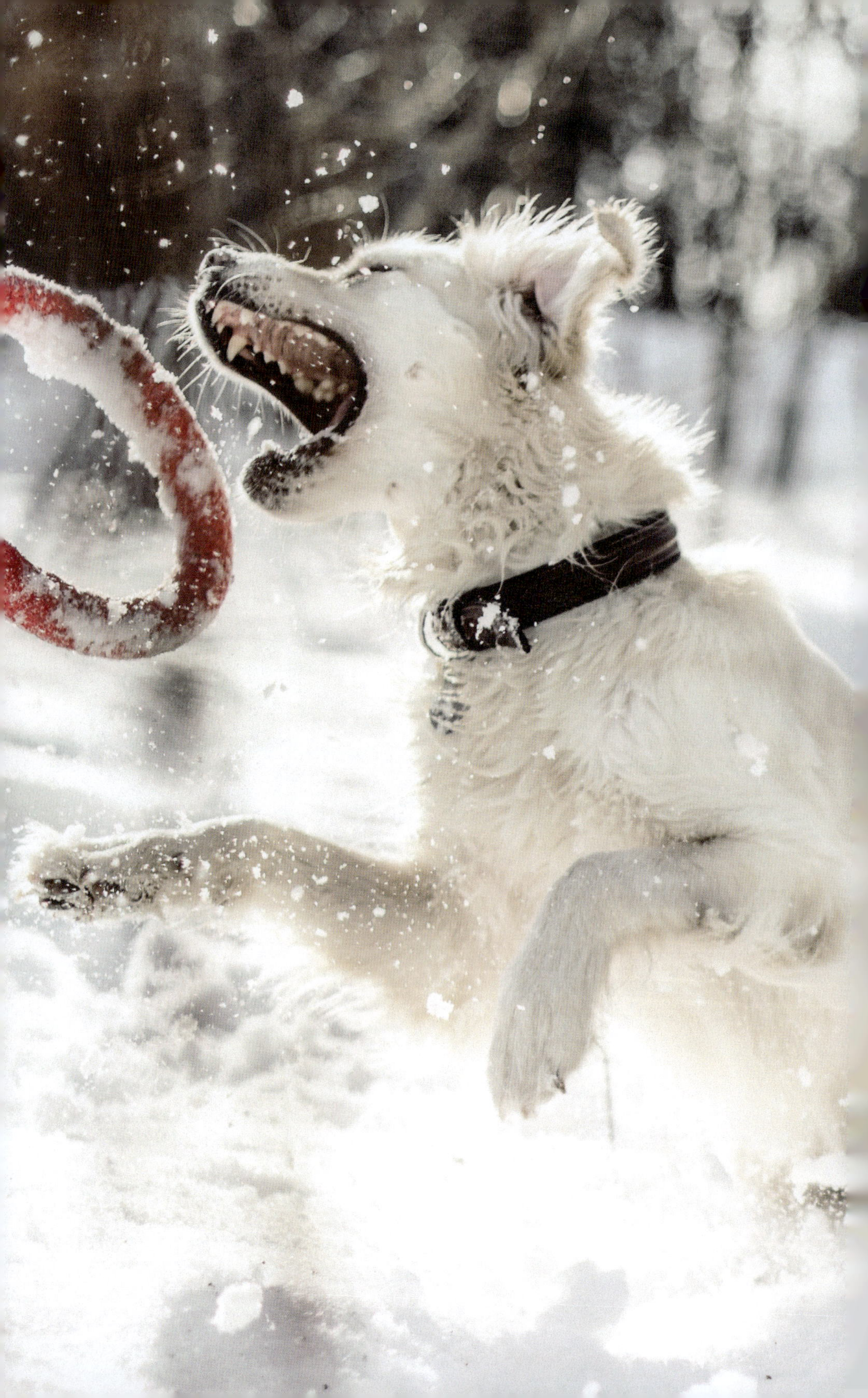

Chapter 4
Good Herbs, "Bad Herbs" And Why *The Right Herbs* Are So Important To Treat The Body And Support The Healing Process.

> *"When your children are teenagers, it's important to have a dog so that someone in the house is happy to see you."*
>
> NORA EPHRON

History and Background of Herbal Medicine

For sixty thousand years herbal medicine has been used to treat symptoms, illnesses and chronic conditions. Herbs, in their purest form are strong *and when prescribed and used properly, have no harmful side effects.*

The oldest written evidence of medicinal plants usage for preparation for drugs has been found on a Sumerian clay slab from Nagpur approximately 5,000 years ago. It comprised of 12 recipes for drug preparation referring to over 250 various plants. The Chinese books of Roots and Grasses by Pen T'Sao written by emperor Shen Nung circa 2500 BC formulated 365 drugs from dried parts of medicinal plants, many of which are still used today.

Ebers papyrus written circa 1550 BC represents a collection of 800 prescriptions referring to hundreds of plant species. In Homer's epic, the Odyssey, created in 800 BC, 63 plants species from the Minoan, Mycenaean, and Egyptian and Assyrian pharmacotherapy were referred to.

The philosopher Hippocrates describes 236 healing herbs and gave precise instruction for herb collection and categorization.

A few hundred years later a Roman army physician, Pedanius Dioscorides, described 600 medicinal volume de-Matre Medica. He specified blossoms, leaves, stems and roots should be collected as well, when herbal remedies are being prepared. His work retained enormous influence for more than 1500 years and was one of the first books printed after the invention of the printing press.

Greek physician and philosopher, Galen (AD130-200) was the court physician to Roman Emperor Marcus Aurelius. He developed the first classification system that paired many common illnesses with their herbal remedy. Galen's writing became the standard for physicians just as the writings of Dioscorides became the standard text for pharmacists. When Rome fell in the 5th century the center of Classical learning moved east to Persia and Constantinople, where Gaelic medicine was enthusiastically adopted and merged with both folk medicine and Egyptian traditions.

This mixture of practices, interwoven with ideas of alchemy, was then reimported back into Europe by traders of invading armies. The most famous Arab physician, Ibn Sina (also known as Avicenna ad 980-1037) wrote the very influential Kitah al-qanun (Canon of medicine), which was firmly based on Galen's principals. By the 12th century this canon had been translated into Latin and brought back to Europe where it became one of the leading text books in the early medical schools.

The use of herbs has been mastered through thousands of years of known results and practices. To master the use of herbs requires a lifetime commitment, requiring meticulous study and research to access the knowledge that has been accumulated over thousands of years, combined with a deep understanding of the animal being treated and their biological needs.

The Unique Healing Power Of Herbs

Herbs have the power to invoke the cleansing and regeneration process that can't be equaled by manufactured supplements or chemical synthetic drugs. Herbs clean and pull toxins from the body while strengthening cells. The uniqueness and superiority of herbs lie in their strong reabsorptive properties.

The restoration properties in herbs enhance, cleanse, and provide nutrition to the cells. Specific herbs have the ability to increase blood and lymph flow within tissues allowing cells to be cleansed and nourished.

The specific mixing of herbs, when combined properly, will achieve what is needed for the body to heal and repair. Herbs are intended for various tissues, glands, organs, as well as systems within the body: the nervous system, digestive system, lymphatic system (immune system), endocrine gland system and blood.

Herbs kill parasites, fungi, harmful bacteria, molds, viruses and worms, while enhancing the immune system.

Note: *Antibiotics only kill bacteria and promote yeast growth. Antibiotics are sulphur based which accumulates in the body causing tissue damage.*

Parasitic herbs also strengthen and repair cells. The great thing about botanicals is that there are no harmful side effects.

I have had great success these many years providing custom tailored herbal formulas for animals who are recovering from chronic and degenerative conditions.

By doing so it allows me to target genetic weaknesses as well as the current condition of the body, while taking into consideration geological location of the animal, weather, environment and lifestyle.

For example:

- Cold air is alkalizing while warm/hot air is less alkalizing. Breathing in alkaline forming air will affect the body differently than breathing in acid forming air.

- Genetic weakness, which is easily detected through the Iridology diagnostic (see chapter on Iridology) will also effect what herbs are needed to support those weaknesses.
- Geological location – what part of the country or in what country is the dog located? What is the average weather temperature, air quality?
- Environment and lifestyle – is the dog living in the city or country? What activities does the dog participate in?

Everything must be taken into consideration when custom formulating herbs to support every single tissue in your dog's body.

These herbal formulas also change to meet the needs and requirements of your dog's ever changing system, while he/she is on this wonderful wellness journey.

I have had many clients tell me "My dog already gets herbs." My question is which herbs are they getting? Many people think of herbs as one big generic cornucopia (they are all the same). That could not be further from the truth. The proper combination is vital in helping your dog achieve optimum levels of health. What is also important is to realize that there are times you will need to change your herbal blends, especially if your dog is trying to recover from a chronic or degenerative condition.

Herbs support is **ESSENTIAL** when your dog is going through a detox. It makes the process so much easier on your dog. The importance of combining herbs with a species - specific diet can be easily compared to a marathon runner. Would you run a marathon in bare feet? In theory it's possible depending on the terrain and how thick and calloused the soles of your feet are. That would be insanity, the proper shoes are critical in the survival and performance of that runner. The herbs act in the very same way. Going without proper herbal support would compare to running a marathon barefoot. You may finish, but it will be a long, hard road to that finish line and what condition will you be in?

The herbs support the detoxification process to make it easier on the body, and in turn make it more gentle and more effective for your dog.

As your dog progresses on a Wellness Program, the formulas need to also progress. This is how to avoid that "plateau effect" - that common issue of "my dog was getting better and then he just stopped - but it helped a little." This is because the herbal formulas need to be altered accordingly. The Iridology is key to recognizing what areas of the body require additional support, as well as 'listening' to your dog's body, taking note of any detox symptoms he is experiencing. The proper herbal support is ever changing to meet your dog's unique requirements at each stage of their life.

"DOGS NEVER BITE ME. JUST HUMANS."

– Marilyn Monroe

Chapter 5

Iridology - A Powerful Diagnostic Tool For Determining The True State Of Your Dog's Health

"There is no psychiatrist in the world like a puppy licking your face."

BEN WILLIAMS

Iridology is a non-invasive way to detect acute, sub-acute, chronic and degenerative conditions in the body. This helps to determine specific herbal and dietary requirements needed to optimize health and wellness.

Gnaz von Peczely, a Hungarian physician, discovered the science of Iridology in 1853, and was responsible for making the science known in Europe. He was also the first to begin mapping out the iris chart.

Some time during his childhood, he accidentally broke the leg of an owl, as he was playing with him. A dark stripe occurred in the 6 o'clock region of the owl's corresponding iris, and Peczely had taken note of this. As he nursed the owl back to health, he discovered that the stripe eventually vanished leaving behind only a little mark. He later went on to study the works of others on the subject of Iridology, and while working as a surgeon, Peczely was able to do comparative research by identifying correlating changes in people's irises and meticulously took note of the changes that occurred, before and after they had gone through surgery.

The iris of the eye is the most complex tissue of the body meeting the outside world. It is an extension of the brain, being incredibly endowed with hundreds of thousands of nerve endings, microscopic blood vessels, muscle and other tissues.

The iris is connected to every organ and tissue of the body by way of the brain and nervous system.

The nerve fibers receive their impulses by way of their connections to the optic nerve, optic thalami and spinal cord. They are formed embryologically from neuroectoderm tissues. Both sympathetic and para-sympathetic nervous systems are present in the iris.

In this way, nature has provided us with a map showing the most remote portions of the body by way of nerve reflex responses. The eye works two ways: not only does it enable us to bring images of the outside world within, it also shows images of what is within, to the outside.

Nerve fibers in the iris respond to changes in body tissues revealing the effects of acidosis in detail by manifesting a reflex physiology that corresponds to specific tissue changes and locations.

It's amazing to watch your dog's health progress by simply looking in the eyes. They will become more clear, less foggy, and even change color. There is no illusion of health when you treat the body, only the reality of health shining through.

Animal Iridology is a powerful tool to help understand the illness and disease in the body based on the various colors and markings in the iris. You can learn more about Iridology - a method of diagnosing the health of the body that dates back to ancient Egypt.

An Equine and Canine Iridology Assessment is the first step used in a WHOLEify Wellness Plan to properly diagnose the health of an animal and determine its genetic weaknesses.

Understanding The Four Stages Of Illness As Reflected In The Iris

There are four key stages of illness - acute, sub-acute, chronic and degenerative. These stages are determined by the level of acidosis within the body. All illness and disease are created by acidic cellular waste caused by stagnation in the lymphatic system, which reveals itself in the iris of an animal.

The iris will show levels of lymphatic build up and deterioration from acidic waste in the body showing up as layers over the eye itself. If your animal's eye is foggy that will show lymphatic buildup throughout the entire system. As the layers of toxicity transition from more chronic to degenerative, the areas of the eye become darker and with a stagnated lymphatic system, may have a cloudy white haze over the entire eye.

Each part of the eye itself represents different areas of the body - a window into that specific area.

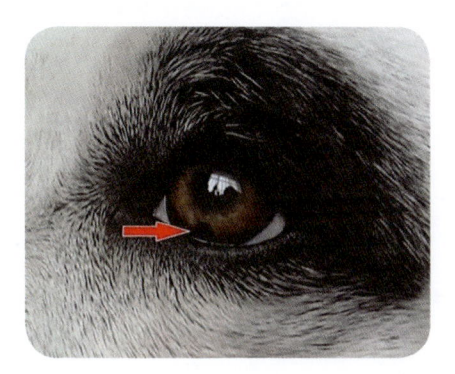

The dog above has kidney weakness - the dark spot shows a degenerative condition that has now formed in the kidneys. Understanding what causes this, and where it's affecting the body, makes recovering from such a condition easier to accomplish.

Treating The Body Not Illness

The body is a complete unit of inner workings made up of chemistry and energy to create its own unique terrain. The terrain is what influences health and wellness. Everything has its own inherent environment in which it can thrive. If the pH is acidic it will provide a perfect breeding ground for harmful bacteria, parasites, fungi, worms, and viruses to thrive.

So let's treat the body through alkaline and detoxification. By doing so, we encourage cellular regeneration.

Treating the body, not the illness, begins with creating an environment in which illness can no longer thrive. This is the reality of health!

It's time to change the tide – together you and I will make a difference to ensure dogs everywhere are no longer suffering needlessly from disease and illness.

Here's to the health of dogs everywhere!

"IF YOU DON'T HAVE A DOG—AT LEAST ONE—THERE IS NOT NECESSARILY ANYTHING WRONG WITH YOU, BUT THERE MAY BE SOMETHING WRONG WITH YOUR LIFE."

- Vincent van Gogh

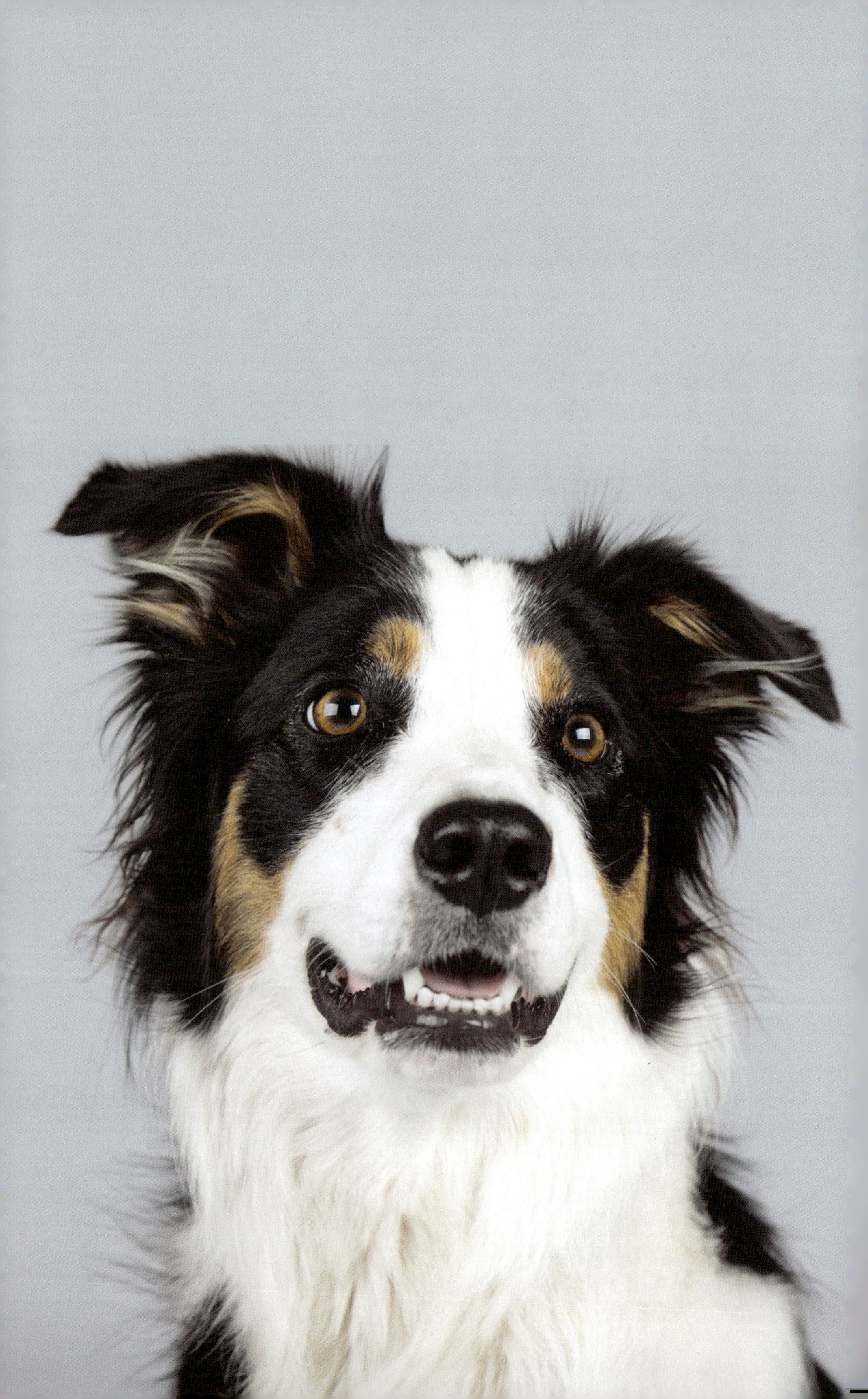

Chapter 6

Transitioning Your Dog To The WHOLEify Way Of Eating

"Ever consider what our dogs must think of us? I mean, here we come back from a grocery store with the most amazing haul: chicken, pork, half a cow. They must think we're the greatest hunters on earth!"

ANNE TYLER

This chapter is the doorway to life-enrichment and well-being for your four-legged best friend.

I recommend a raw beef marrow bone for your dog to chew on no matter what age.

If your dog is eating a conventional, processed food diet then we will want to transition your dog onto a natural raw diet. I like to begin the transition with chicken soup. Cooked foods are acidic, but much less than that of processed foods. So this is the reason we take that first step. We don't want your dog to detox too quickly so we need to alkaline the system methodically.

I also recommend coconut water, nut milks and smoothies. See recipes and health benefits.

Step 1. Remove all processed foods.
Step 2. Make chicken soup.
Step 3. Have good raw beef bones available.
Step 4. Stock up on fresh whole foods.

WHOLEify Your Dog With RAW Natural Foods

List Of Natural Foods For Your Dog

A must have - RAW Beef Marrow Bones

Meat

- Beef, Chicken, Turkey, Lamb, Bison, or Venison
- **NO PORK.** Pigs are omnivores, you do not want to feed your dog the same species of animal.

Veggies

- Carrots, Broccoli, Pumpkin, Green beans, Peas, Avocado, Zucchini, Cucumber, Leafy Greens and any seasonal veggie they may like.

Fruit

- Apples, Pears, Melon, Berries, Grapes, Banana, Mango, Papaya, Persimmons, any seasonal fruit they may like.

Nuts

- Almonds, Pecans, Cashews, Walnuts.

Seeds

- Pumpkin seeds, Sunflower seeds, Hemp seeds.

Dried Fruit (without sweetener)

- Cranberries, Coconut flakes, Goji berries, Dates, Banana, Apricots.

Oils

- Coconut oil

Drinks

- Filtered or bottled water, nut milks, coconut water, and smoothies. *(See recipes)*

Transition Menu

Day 1-3

Breakfast	Lunch	Dinner	Snack
Bowl of chicken soup in a separate dish	Bowl of chicken soup in separate dish	Bowl of Chicken soup	Any of the following:
1 Scoop WHOLEify Wellness Herbal Blend.	Add in any of the listed fruits, nuts and seeds from list with 2-4 oz coconut water.	In separate dish choose any of the following veggies nuts and seeds from the list.	Smoothie or almond milk with fruit and nuts/seeds - or a smoothie bowl for your dog.
1t Coconut oil			
In a separate dish choose any of the following fruits: nuts and seeds from the feeding list or add the nutty bowl - or a smoothie bowl. *See recipes.*	Provide your dog with a raw beef marrow bone to chew freely.		

47

Day 4-5

Breakfast	Lunch	Dinner	Snack
Bowl of soup	Small dish of raw ground meat .	Bowl of soup	Choose from the recipe list.
In a separate dish	Add in any of the veggies from the list.	In separate bowl choose any of the following veggies, nuts and seeds from the list.	Smoothie or almond milk with fruit, nuts and seeds or smoothie bowl for your dog.
1t Coconut oil			
1 Scoop *WHOLEify* Immune Enhancer Herbal Formula			
Choose any of the fruits, nuts and seeds from the list or make your puppy a nutty bowl or a smoothie bowl.	Provide your dog with a raw marrow bone to chew freely.		

Transitioning Your Dog To The Wholeify Way Of Eating

Fruits, vegetables, eggs and raw beef – another delicious raw meal.

Day 6-7

Breakfast	Lunch	Dinner	Snack
Raw ground meat	Chicken soup	Raw meat	Choose any
1 Scoop *WHOLEify* K9 Immune Emhancer Herbal Formula	In a separate dish	Choose any veggies buts and seeds from the list.	smoothie, or a dog smoothie bowl almond milk, any fruits nuts or seeds from the list.
1t coconut oil	Choose any fruits, nuts and seeds from the list		
Choose from any of the fruits, nuts and seeds from the list	Provide dog with a raw marrow bone to chew freely.		

Day 8 - All Natural Diet

Key Ingredients That Are A "Must Have" Daily.

WHOLEify Organic Wellness Herbs For Dogs - to ensure the body is supported at all times. All our blends are made of all organic human grade superfoods and botanicals to promote health in your dog throughout their life.

Recommended Product: WHOLEify Immune Enhancer

Why?:

- disease preventative
- anti parasitic (daily wormer)
- anti- fungal
- anti- viral
- supports joint health and healthy circulation
- supports healthy digestion
- glandular support
- organ support.

(See promo code at the back of this book to save on WHOLEify Immune Enhancer™)

Raspberry, Dates, Lamb & Coconut – A Gourmet Raw Meal

Coconut oil

Coconut oil has an abundance of health benefits including digestive health, anti bacterial, and alkalizing properties. Coconut oil contains ketones which provide energy to the brain promoting focus and memory.

The following list would be good for your dog to have a 2-3 times a week:

1. **Coconut water** - Coconut water is extremely hydrating/alkaline. It contains an enormous amount of vitamins and minerals that promote immune health.
2. **Nut milks** - Nut milks are very nourishing containing high levels of Vitamin E along with Vitamin D and healthy fats.

Changes You Will Notice While Your Dog Is On A Natural Raw Food Diet

- They will drink less. This diet provides hydration on a cellular level. Alkaline = hydration.
- Dogs' stool will turn white and powdery within days and disappear. It is "biodegradable" so no more picking up doggie-doo in the backyard.
- Your dog's will maintain healthy white teeth and gums - brushing their teeth is not necessary.
- They will attract less flies, fleas and ticks.
- A natural diet prevents harmful worms and parasites who thrive in an acid environment. When your dog is eating naturally they maintain a perfect pH balance.
- Makes training a lot easier, your dog will have better focus with an overall calm awareness.

"I WANT TO BECOME THE PERSON MY DOG THINKS I AM."

Chapter 7
Healing Food & Delicious Homemade Treat Recipes

"Such short little lives our pets have to spend with us, and they spend most of it waiting for us to come home each day."

JOHN GROGAN

Here are some of my favorite tried and tested home-made recipes that I recommend to my clients and make regularly for my own four dogs at home.

Chicken Soup

- Chicken thighs or boneless breast meat
- Carrots
- 4 dime sized slices of Ginger Root
- Parsley

* Place in a large pot of water and bring to a boil. Then reduce heat and simmer for about 1 hour.

Nutty Bowl

This meal contains a variety of fruits, veggies, nuts and seeds for a complete meal. You can just about mix any fruit or veggies together in the food processor and add maple syrup, nuts, dates, coconut butter, vanilla and cinnamon. Blend until it looks like oatmeal. This meal is very nourishing for dogs of all ages. This meal is especially good for older dogs who may have trouble chewing.

Ingredients:
- 1   Apple
- 1   Banana
- 1   Carrot
- 4   Dates (pitted)
- 1T   Coconut Butter
- ¼C   Maple Syrup
- 1T   Vanilla
- 1t   Cinnamon
- Handful Raisins
- Flaxseed meal
- Hemp seed
- Walnuts
- Pecans
- Cashews
- Sunflower seeds

Cherry Berry Smoothie

This is a great snack between meals that is both nourishing and hydrating while providing antioxidants to support the immune system.

Ingredients:
- Almond Milk
- Fresh Cherries With Pits Removed
- Fresh Strawberries

- Fresh Blueberries
- Fresh Banana
- Vanilla

*   Blend until smooth.

Trail Mix

K9 Trail mix is a blend of pecans, almonds, cashews, walnuts, sunflower seeds, coconut flakes and dried cranberries. It's the perfect between-meal snack as well as a good training treat! Also great to take along on a hike, boating, or on a trip.

Smoothie Bowl

Ingredients:
- ¼C Fresh mixed Berries/ Cherries
- 4oz Unsweetened Almond Milk
- 1T Unsweetened Almond Butter
- 1T Maple Syrup or Honey
- ½ Banana
- Hemp Seed
- Sliced Almonds
- Coconut Flakes
- Sunflower Seeds
- Pumpkin Seeds
- Goji Berries

1. Place berries, almond milk, almond butter, maple syrup or honey and 1/2 banana in blender and blend until smooth.
2. Place smoothie in bowl.
3. Top with hemp seeds, sliced almonds, coconut flakes, sunflower seeds, pumpkin seeds and goji berries.

Healthy Raw Treat Recipes

Almond Kisses

Ingredients:
- 1C   Organic Almonds
- ½C   Pecans
- 8-10   Organic pitted Medjool Dates
- 1T   Vanilla
- 1t   Sea Salt
- ½C   Organic Unsweetened Almond Butter
- 3T   Coconut Oil
- ¼C   Maple Syrup

1. Place almonds, pitted medjool dates, vanilla, sea salt and maple syrup in a food processor and blend.
2. Place blended dough in large bowl and set aside.
3. Place almond butter and coconut oil in a small sauce pan and on a very low heat melt together.
4. Pour the coconut oil/almond butter over the "blended dough mixture".
5. Mix together.
6. Line a small cake pan with parchment paper and add the dough.
7. Press the dough firmly in pan so it fills each corner evenly.
8. Cover with plastic wrap and place in the freezer for 2 hours
9. Remove from freezer and cut even slices of treats.
10. You can keep treats in freezer until ready to feed/ if you want to keep some in the fridge they stay good for about 2 weeks.

Sunshine Cookies

Ingredients:
- ¼C Almonds
- 1T Chia Seeds
- 1t Hemp Seeds
- 1T Ground Flaxseed
- 1T Sunflower Seeds
- 9 Pitted Medjool Dates
- 5 Dried Apricots (Chopped)
- 1T Shredded Coconut
- 1T Pumpkin Seeds
- 1t Sea Salt
- ½t Cinnamon

1. Place dates, apricots, in a food processor and blend into a paste.
2. Add almonds, sea salt and cinnamon and blend leaving the almonds chunky.
3. Place dough in a bowl and add remaining ingredients.
4. Mix with your hands and shape into small cookies.
5. Refrigerate or freeze - stays good for 3 days in fridge.

Peanut Butter Pooches

Ingredients:
- 1C Organic Pecans
- ½C Sunflower Seeds
- ¼C Organic Almonds
- 8-10 Organic Pitted Medjool Dates
- 1T Vanilla
- 1t Sea Salt
- ½C Organic unsweetened Peanut Butter
- 3T Coconut Oil
- ¼C Maple Syrup

1. Place pecans, sunflower seeds, almonds, pitted medjool dates, vanilla, sea salt and maple syrup in a food processor and blend.
2. Place blended dough in large bowl and set aside
3. Place peanut butter and coconut oil in a small sauce pan and on a very low heat. Melt together.
4. Pour the coconut oil/peanut butter over the "blended dough mixture".
5. Mix together.
6. Line a small cake pan with parchment paper and add the dough
7. Press the dough firmly in pan so it fills each corner evenly
8. Cover with plastic wrap and place in the freezer for 2 hours
9. Remove from freezer and cut even slices of treats.

You can keep treats in freezer until ready to feed. If you want to keep some in the fridge they stay good for about 2 weeks.

"A HOUSE IS NOT A HOME UNTIL IT HAS A DOG."

– Gerald Durrell

Chapter 8
Natural Remedies & First Aid

"I think dogs are the most amazing creatures; they give unconditional love. For me, they are the role models for being alive."

GILDA RADNER

Diet plays a key role in healing the body no matter what injury or illness your dog is suffering from. Feeding your dog, a natural, alkaline forming diet will enhance the healing ability in the body. Alkaline chemistry is the healing side of chemistry, repairing damage to the body. Cellular regeneration begins internally. Animals will heal much faster when they are eating a natural species friendly diet.

Being prepared is always helpful. Dogs tend to get in trouble when we least expect it.

Below is a list of essentials to have just in case.

NATURAL & USEFUL HOME ESSENTIALS FOR DOGS

1. Black Walnut Hull powder
2. Yarrow (cut and sifted or powder form)
3. Oregano oil capsule
4. Manuka Honey
5. Colloidal Silver
6. Apple Cider Vinegar
7. Activated Charcoal Capsules
8. Miracle 2 Soap
9. Dr Bronner's Pure-Castile Soap – Peppermint
10. Liquid Benadryl

1. Black Walnut Hull powder has been used throughout history for thousands of years to treat an array of issues. But it is most commonly known to fight intestinal parasites. Black walnut is most effective against pinworm, ringworm, tapeworm, and other intestinal parasites.

   Black walnut hull is also anti-fungal and anti-bacterial. It is great to use both internally and externally as well.

2. Yarrow has been a "first aid" plant/herb for eons.

   Achilles used it to treat the wounds of his men. Today, historians and botanists agree that the herb described in Homer's Iliad was yarrow. Centuries may have passed, but yarrow has not lost its effectiveness. Yarrow has very potent healing properties. .

   I have used yarrow internally as well as externally. I once used it on a client's horse who had punctured her Iris. The veterinarian wanted to remove the horse's eye. I asked my client to give me 24 hours with her horse. I applied my own proprietary blend of yarrow tea to the eye every 15 minutes for the first two hours. Then had my client apply yarrow tea drops in the eye every hour. The very next day the horse's eye was healed to the shock and amazement of many. It is also good to note that yarrow stops bleeding internally as well as externally. When in doubt use yarrow!

3. Vitamin E oil is a fat-soluble antioxidant which fights off free radicals as well as having anti-inflammatory properties. It is well known that Vitamin E repairs tissue damage.

4. Oregano Oil capsules are best known for being a very powerful natural antibiotic. Oregano oil contains the following:

   > Carvacrol – The most abundant phenol in oregano oil. According to Heathline it has been shown to stop the growth of several different types of bacteria.

   > Thymol - Antifungal that can also support the immune system and protects against harmful toxins.

> Rosmarinic Acid: is a powerful antioxidant that helps protect against damage caused by toxins/free radicals.

Georgetown University researchers have found that oregano oil is an effective treatment against dangerous and sometimes drug resistant bacteria. Two of the studies have shown oregano oil to reduce infection more effectively than traditional antibiotics.

Oregano oil was tested by the Biotics Research Corporation and was proven effective against Giardia, which is an intestinal parasite. Good to note that traditional antibiotics are non-effective against this parasite.

5. Manuka Honey - For thousands of years honey has been used to treat wounds, burns, and sores. In 2007 Manuka honey was approved by the US FDA as an option for wound treatment.

   Honey offers antibacterial and antioxidant properties, all the while providing a protective barrier to prevent microbial infections.

   Multiple studies have shown that Manuka honey can enhance wound healing, amplify the regeneration of tissue, and even decrease pain from abrasions and burns.

6. Colloidal Silver has powerful antibacterial, anti-fungal and anti-viral properties. Studies show that colloidal silver has a broad-spectrum antimicrobial agent that may be able to fight and kill pathogens. It can inhibit the growth of both aerobic (requiring oxygen) and anaerobic (not requiring oxygen) bacteria, according to research published in the Journal of Alternative and Complementary Medicine.
   Colloidal Silver works to soothe minor skin conditions because of its potent anti-fungal properties and its ability to soothe the skin, while repairing tissue damage.

   Note: *I have found it to be very effective on eye injuries to prevent infection and to aid in the healing process. It is also very soothing in the eye.*

7. Apple Cider Vinegar has been used for many homeopathic remedies throughout the centuries. It is known to kill pathogens including harmful bacteria. It is traditionally used for cleaning and disinfecting, treating fungus, lice, and ear infections.

    Note: *Hippocrates used it for wound cleaning over two thousand years ago.*

8. Activated Charcoal – is a fine, odorless, black powder often used in emergency rooms to treat overdoses. It's toxin-absorbing properties have a wide range of medicinal purposes. Giving your dog activated charcoal will help with stomach aches, gas, and diarrhea. I also like to use it topically on wounds as an antibacterial. It is also good to give your dog a capsule if they have been stung or bitten by a spider to help absorb any poisons. Note: Activated charcoal is pretty powerful 1 capsule is usually plenty when using internally.

9. Liquid Benadryl – I only recommend this for emergency poisonous snake bites or allergic reactions to a bite/sting of any kind. You want to give 1mg per pound of body weight or 1tsp. per every 12.5 pounds of body weight.

INJURIES / FIRST AID

Cuts and Abrasions

I <u>NEVER</u> recommend covering a wound. In my twenty plus years of experience I've found wounds heal quickly without risk of infection when the wound is treated instead with the proper herbal application and left open to drain and heal without trapping in bacteria or creating a moist environment in which bacteria can thrive.

The idea is to create a healing environment in which the body can heal. This holds true for both internal and external healing.

Skin Surface Scratched and/or Scraped

1. Mix Miracle 2 soap in a bowl of warm water and gently sponge on the wound. Do not rinse.

   Note: *Diluted Miracle 2 soap does not require rinsing.*

2. Place black walnut hull powder directly on wound and leave to heal.
3. Repeat daily as needed.

Hair Matted Around Wound

1. Mix Miracle 2 soap in a bowl of warm water.
2. Gently cleanse the wound and loosen the hair the best you can around the wound.
3. Very carefully cut fur away from wound so the wound area is open and exposed.
4. Make a clean bowl of Miracle 2 warm soapy water and gently clean the wound again. Do not rinse.
5. Rub a thin layer of manuka honey on wound.
6. Place black walnut hull powder over honey and leave uncovered.
7. Repeat daily until wound is healed.

8. If wound has puss in it – give your dog oregano oil capsules once a day for 10 days. Oregano oil is a very powerful natural anti- biotic.

   Dosage
   10 – 25 pounds   1 capsule 1 x day
   25-45 lbs.   1 capsule 2 x day
   45 – 60 lbs.   2 capsules in the morning and 1 capsule at night
   60 lbs. and up   2 capsules 2 x day.

Bleeding - Difficult to Stop

1. Yarrow tea will stop the bleeding.

   3T of cut and sifted organic yarrow to 1 cup hot water.
   a. Seep for 15 minutes then strain.
   b. With a clean cotton ball apply yarrow tea to wound (make sure it is warm and not hot).
   c. Apply every 2 minutes until bleeding stops/slows down.

2. Make a poultice for wound.

   a. In a small glass container or bowl place two parts walnut hull powder to approximately one part, Vitamin E oil.
   b. You will want to create a poultice that is wet enough to stick but not too wet that is runs off. You want the poultice to stick to the wound nicely.
   c. If your dog licks it off just re-apply. Vitamin E is a natural antiseptic and contains many internal and external healing properties. Black walnut hull is nature's most powerful anti - parasitic, anti - bacteria, and anti - fungal herb in the botanical family.

Puncture Wounds

1. Mix Miracle 2 soap in a bowl of warm water.
2. Gently cleanse the wound.
3. Place a thin layer of manuka honey on wound.
4. Place black walnut hull powder over manuka honey.
5. Repeat daily until wound is healed.
6. Give your dog oregano oil capsules once a day for 10 days to prevent infection. Oregano oil is a very powerful natural anti-biotic.

   Dosage
   10 – 25 pounds   1 capsule 1 x day
   25-45 lbs.   1 capsule 2 x day
   45 – 60 lbs.   2 capsules in the morning and 1 capsule at night
   60 lbs. and up   2 capsules 2 x day.

Maggots in Wound

1. Clean wound with Miracle 2 soap and warm water – do not rinse.
2. Remove the maggots that are in view.
3. Apply black walnut hull powder to wound and leave for 10 minutes.
4. Apply poultice over the black walnut hull powder and leave open do not wrap wound.

   Poultice for wound:
   a. In a small glass container or bowl place two parts Walnut hull powder to approximately one part, Vitamin E oil.
   b. You will want to create a poultice that is wet enough to stick but not too wet that is runs off. You want the poultice to stick to the wound nicely.
   c. If your dog licks it off just re-apply. Vitamin E is a natural anti septic and contains many internal and external healing properties. Black walnut hull is nature's most powerful anti–parasitic, anti-bacteria, and anti-fungal herb in the botanical family.

5. Give your dog oregano oil capsules for 10 days.

Dosage

25 pounds	1 capsule 1 x day
25-45 lbs.	1 capsule 2 x day
45 – 60 lbs.	2 capsules in the morning and 1 capsule at night
60 lbs. +	2 capsules 2 x day. For 10 days.

Eye Injuries

Eye injuries are very common in dogs. The eye is very sensitive. Applying gentle and soothing healing methods are most important.

I like to use Yarrow Tea and/or Colloidal Silver for eyes.

1. Yarrow tea is made by adding 2-4 Tbs. of cut and sifted organic yarrow in 1 cup of hot water. Allow to seep for 20 minutes.
2. Strain and use.
3. You can keep yarrow tea in the refrigerator for up to 2 weeks.

Minor Eye Injuries - Apply one dropper full of colloidal silver initially to injured eye. Wait 10 minutes then apply 1 dropper of yarrow tea 3 x day.

Swollen Eye – Apply one dropper of colloidal silver. Wait 10 minutes, then soak a soft cotton cloth in yarrow tea and hold gently on eye for 1 -2 minutes 3 x day.

Eye Injury (cut or abrasion) - Apply one dropper full colloidal silver. Wait 10 minutes then apply one dropper of Yarrow tea in eye. Repeat every 15 minutes for 1 hour. Then continue with Yarrow tea every hour for 4-6 hours.

If eye is still irritated the next day:
- Apply 1 dropper colloidal silver. Wait 10 minutes and apply 1 dropper yarrow tea every hour until eye begins to look healthy.
- Give your dog oregano oil capsules for 7 days.

Dosage

10 – 25 lbs.	1 capsule 1 x day
25-45 lbs.	1 capsule 2 x day
45 – 60 lbs.	2 capsules in the morning and 1 capsule at night
60 lbs. and up	2 capsules 2 x day.

Nail Bleeding

Whether you accidently cut your dog's nails too short and hit the wick or your dog pulled off a part of his/her nail by accident, the best way to take care of this is to:

1. Soak his/her paw in a bowl of yarrow tea to slow the bleeding.
2. Place black walnut hull powder on the nail.

Ear Mites

Apple cider vinegar works best to get rid of ear mites.
1. Soak a cotton ball in apple cider vinegar and gently clean your dog's ears
2. Only clean the part of the ear, you can see.
3. Then with a small dropper place a small drop of Apple Cider Vinegar in the ear, NOT in the canal, only in the area of the ear you can see.
4. Do this daily until mites are no longer an issue.

Water In The Ears

After a bath, or swimming in the lake or ocean, it is always good to take a cotton swab soaked in hydrogen peroxide and gently clean out your dog's ears. The peroxide will remove the water and prevent ear infections again. Make sure you only clean the area of the ear you can see.

Tick Bites

After removing the tick (use tweezers or your fingernails to ensure you remove the head of the tick), apply a small amount of apple cider vinegar to the bite area and sprinkle a little activated charcoal on it.

Snake Bites

Immediately give your dog liquid Benadryl - 1tsp. per every 12.5 pounds of body weight. After 15 minutes give your dog activated charcoal in capsule form (hide the capsules in a small piece of cheese or banana).

20-60 pounds	1 capsule
60 pounds +	2 capsules of activated charcoal.

Natural Remedies for Common Aliments

Diarrhea

If your dog has diarrhea, give your dog pumpkin and bananas.

1. The organic natural 100% pumpkin for pies with no sugar added is great to always have on hand. Pumpkins contain a variety of powerful healing qualities. One of them being a natural antioxidant. Pumpkin destroys harmful bacteria which cause the diarrhea.
2. You will also want to make sure your dog stays hydrated. In this case where his/her tummy is upset, the banana is soothing and contains high level potassium to hydrate the body.
3. I recommend to my clients to make a Ginger Chicken Broth to sooth their tummy. Ingredients – Chicken breast (organic or natural with no antibiotics added), filtered water (or spring water), and fresh ginger (one root). Grate the ginger or dice. Allow the soup to simmer for 1 hour.
4. Coconut Water is another great way to hydrate your dog and to replace electrolytes. Give it to them in a separate bowl next to their water dish.
5. Give 1 capsule Activated Charcoal once a day for 2 days.

Constipation

If your dog becomes constipated, feed them fresh papaya and give them coconut water – lots of coconut water to drink (note this is coconut water not coconut milk). After they drink the coconut water and eat the papaya, take them out for a good long walk and run.

Stomach and Ulcers

If your dog has an upset tummy, make them a cup of Chamomile Tea (just add boiling water to the tea bag and let it sit for 5 minutes to draw in the flavor). Just remember to add cold water to it before giving it to your dog so they don't get burned! Add it to their (raw) food. Give your dog fresh papaya and banana in their meal.

If your dog has a nervous ulcerated tummy, add lots of fresh papaya to their raw meals. Papaya contains high levels of vitamin K and the enzyme Papain which assists in healing ulcerations.

The **WHOLEify K9 Immune Enhancer**™ will help the body to accelerate its repair and healing process. Visit www.WHOLEify.com (See promo code at back of book)

Allergies & Hot Spots

If your dog has allergies, switching them over to a natural raw diet will help alleviate your dog's discomfort and reduce the amount of scratching and inflammation. Skin, in effect, is the third and largest kidney in the body. Your dog is suffering from skin issues because your dog is actually detoxing. Their body is trying to rid itself of the harmful toxins. We must support them through that detox process so their body can eliminate the acidic cellular waste, which is happening through the "third kidney" - the skin.

Here's how to best support your dog:

1. Immediately change your dog's diet to an all-natural, raw, specific diet as explained earlier in this book. Everything is cause and effect. In order to change the effect, in this case, being red irritated itchy skin and hot spots, we must alter the cause. The cause usually stems from what is being consumed. Changing the diet to a species friendly diet will enhance the immune system allowing the rest of the toxins to filter out through the kidneys.
2. Give your dog one tablespoon of **K9 Immune Enhancer**™ twice a day with their food (visit www.WHOLEify.com). This herbal-super-food-power-blend will accelerate the dog's ability to heal and provide extra support to its immune system which is much needed.
3. Shampoo your dog with Dr. Bronner's Castile Peppermint Soap. (Make sure NOT to get the soap near your dog's eyes). Rinse well. This will relieve and cool down the skin, while washing away the toxins that the skin has already eliminated.

Infected Ears

A dog's ear is very tender especially if it is infected.

Signs of an ear infection:

- Swelling and inflammation
- Ears are hot around the skin
- Bad odor
- Discharge
- Interior of ear is red
- Skin is crusty
- Pain when ear is touched
- Ear wax is dark
- Your dog is protecting his ear.

The first thing you need to do is gently clean your dog's ear. When cleaning your dog's ears, you only want to clean the part of the ear that you can see.

NEVER dig deep into a dog's ear canal.

Here's how to clean them:
1. Mix 1 part apple cider vinegar to 4 parts yarrow tea.
2. Soak a cotton ball in your natural ear solution and gently clean your dog's ear.
3. Clean your dog's ear with the yarrow vinegar solution 2-3 times a day.
4. Give your dog oregano oil capsules, twice a day with meals for 10 days.

Dosage

10 – 25 lbs.	1 capsule 1 x day
25-45 lbs.	1 capsule 2 x day
45 – 60 lbs.	2 capsules in the morning and 1 capsule at night
60 lbs. and up	2 capsules 2 x day.

"MY CATS INSPIRE ME DAILY. THEY INSPIRE ME TO GET A DOG!"

— Greg Curtis

Bonus Chapter
Chapter 9
WHOLEify YOUR Puppy

"Handle every situation like a dog. If you can't eat it or play with it, just pee on it and walk away."

AUTHOR UNKNOWN

So you have a new puppy! Congratulations!

This is the perfect opportunity to make sure your puppy grows up healthy and strong! All our WHOLEify puppies have the benefit of starting off healthy and sustaining optimum levels of wellness!

Bringing home a new puppy is very exciting but you will want to make sure to have a few things prepared before you bring home your little one.

List of things to have before bringing home your puppy

- WHOLEify Puppy Herbal Formula™ (See promo code at back of this book)
- Bed
- Blanket
- Crate
- Food / water bowl
- Puppy harness and leash – puppies should always start out in a harness, never a choker chain.
- Toys
- Beef marrow bones
- Stock up on fresh whole food!

Grocery Store List

- Beef marrow bones
- Boneless chicken
- Carrot
- Ginger root
- Parsley
- Apple
- Banana
- Avocado
- Fresh vegetables – peas, green beans etc.
- Coconut oil
- Almond milk
- Coconut water
- Almonds
- Pecans
- Dates
- Maple syrup
- Coconut flakes
- Cranberries

You will want to start your puppy off on chicken soup for the first week. This is to ensure a good transition from your breeder/adoption agency to their new home.

The chicken soup is a great way to get your puppy started on a healthy diet.

Ingredients:
- 4-5 Boneless chicken breast
- 2 carrots
- 4 slices of fresh ginger root
- Handful of parsley

Directions:
* Place ingredients in a large pot of water and let simmer for about an hour.

I like to make enough to last at least a few days. Depending on how big your puppy is you will have to decide on portions. Remember it is nourishing food.

On Day 5 begin introducing raw meat. Just give your puppy a small amount of ground meat in with some fruits and veggies.

On Day 7 your puppy is ready for a complete raw food diet.

Tater enjoying her #WHOLEify dinner

WHOLEify Your Dog

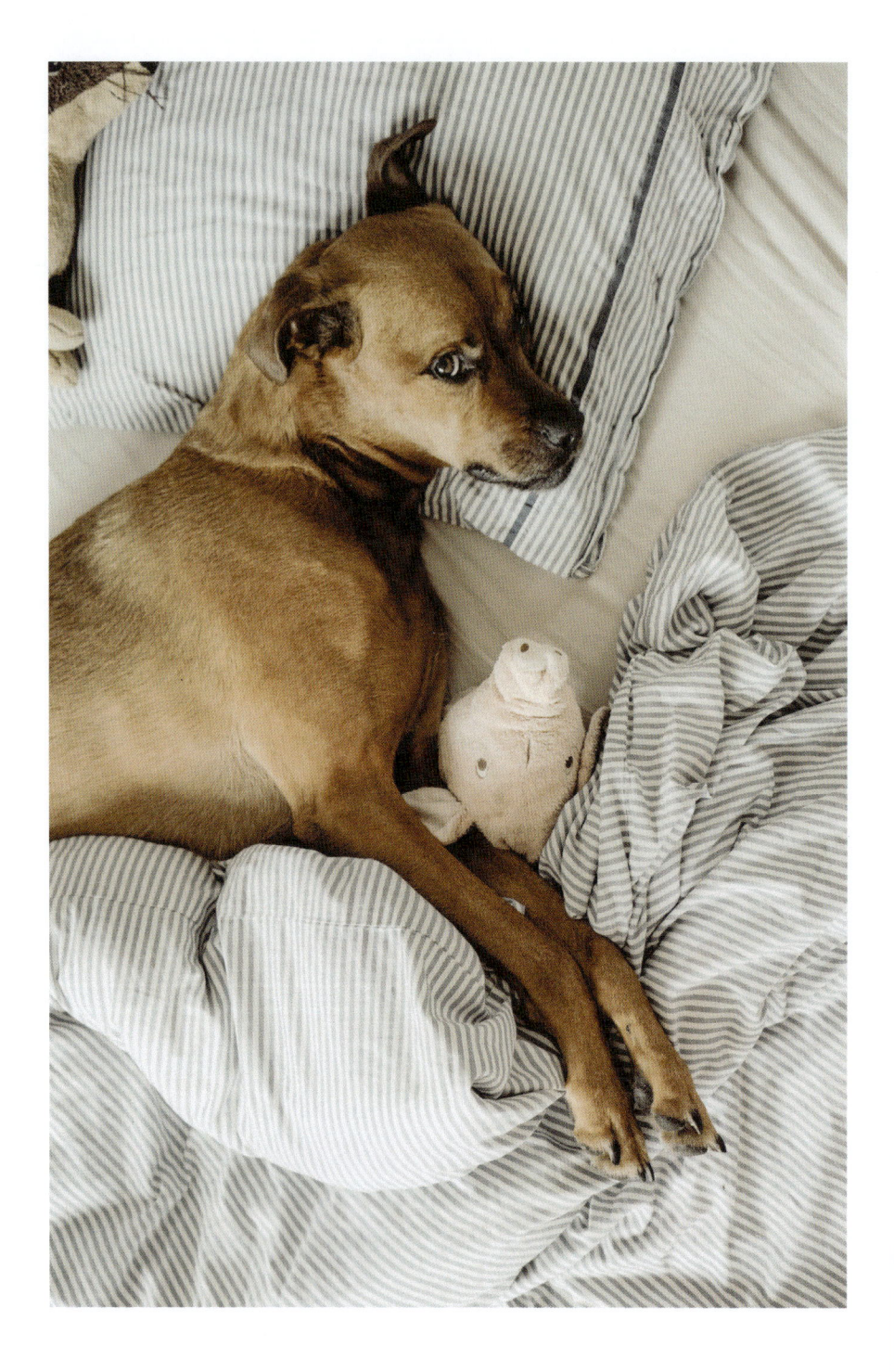

Complete Raw Food Diet For Your Puppy And Feeding Routines

Puppies need to eat small, frequent meals.

I recommend:

8 – 14 weeks	4 meals a day
14- 18 weeks	3 meals a day
5 months and up	2 meals a day with 2 small snacks.

Switch them over to the WHOLEify dog feeding regime in chapter 9.

Meet Athena, a #WHOLEify puppy who has been on a custom #WHOLEify program since birth

Seasonal feeding is important, as is variety. Puppies love food, so take advantage of this time to introduce them to a delicious assortment of seasonal fruits and veggies. Feeding a variety of foods on a daily basis ensures your puppy is getting the optimum levels of vitamins and minerals to grow healthy and strong. It is not healthy for a puppy to consume the same thing day after day. We would not feed our children a bowl of cereal everyday for the rest of their lives. They would be malnourished.

Have fun with the natural diet - your puppy deserves the best nature has to offer.

You will want to make sure your puppy always has a bone to chew on. Beef marrow bones will save you hundreds of dollars on replacing shoes, clothing, furniture and yes, even the walls of your house.

It's never too early to start training your new puppy

1. Create designated sleeping and eating routines to help him acclimatize to his new home.
2. Choose wisely where your new puppy will sleep. It is important that he can see family life with suitable dog bedding to sleep in.
3. Choose a place for him to eat with enough room for food.
4. Always ensure fresh water is available

Choosing a name for your puppy

A short, 2-3 syllable name will avoid confusion with single-syllable commands.

- Names should be short. A 2-3 syllable name is best because it is brief and will not be confused with one-syllable commands such as "No" or "Sit".
- Be consistent. All family members should use the same name for the puppy.
- Start training your puppy to sit, stay, and come.

Getting your dog to come to you when called is the most important command to teach them, it can save their life one day.

During the first few months, puppies really benefit from a good routine, so get into the habit of feeding your puppy at regular intervals. Take them outside as soon as they wake up, following their mealtimes, and every hour or two. Make sure that you schedule in 'play times', and 'quiet times' when you are present. Your puppy needs to learn to settle quietly as well as how to occupy themselves with a chew or toys.

But most of all enjoy your puppy and, if you are like me and have several large dogs, enjoy the short time you are able to pick them up and hug them because it won't be long before they are much too big to do that!

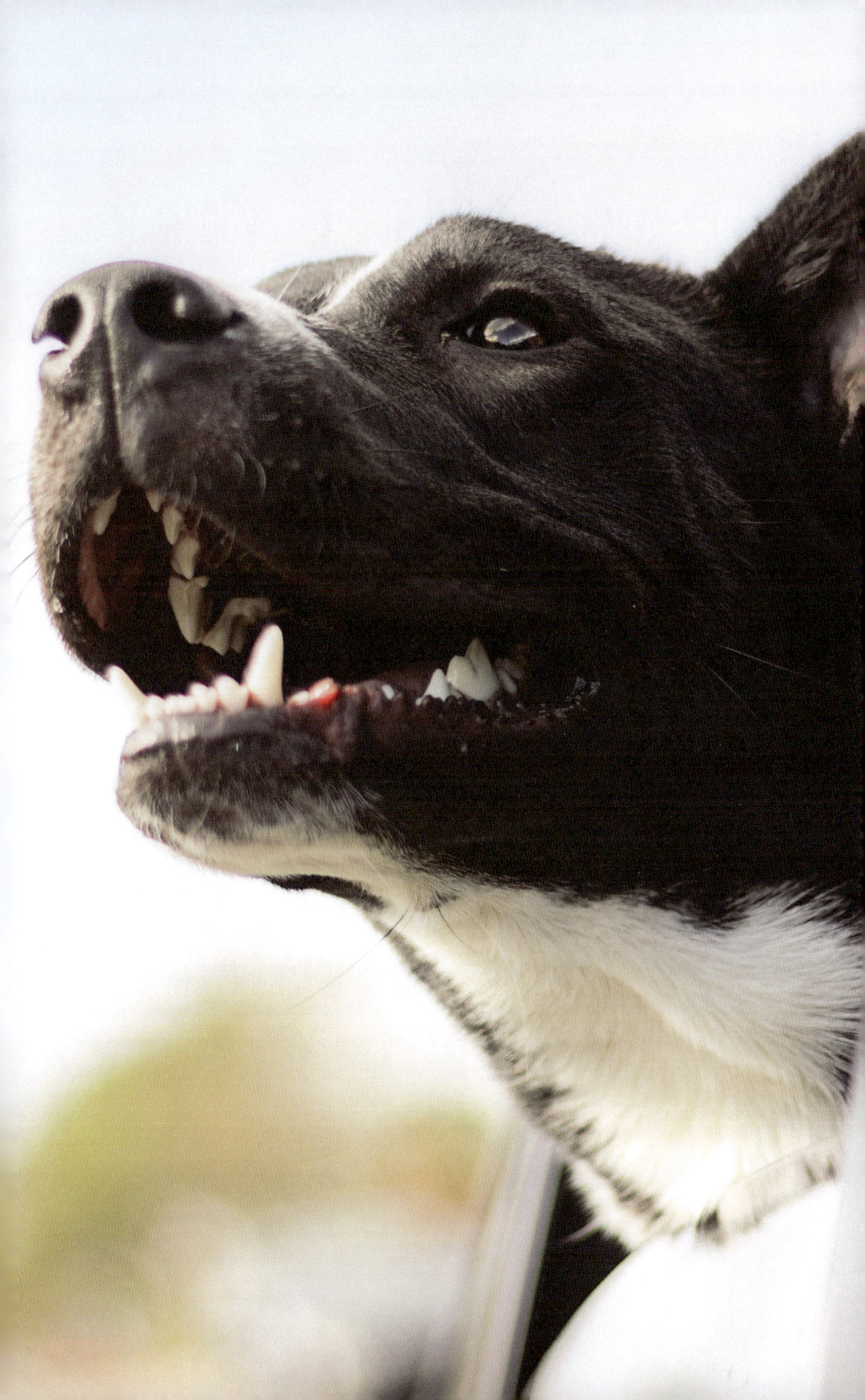

"DOGS FEEL VERY STRONGLY THAT THEY SHOULD ALWAYS GO WITH YOU IN THE CAR, IN CASE THE NEED SHOULD ARISE FOR THEM TO BARK VIOLENTLY AT NOTHING RIGHT IN YOUR EAR."

- Dave Barry

CONCLUSION

Well there you have it – we have reached the end of the book but I hope not the end of our journey together. Congratulations on taking this very important first step in restoring your dog back to whole health.

"What's next?", you may be asking?
Now it's your turn. You have an important choice to make.

Will you:

a) Say "thanks Lisa for the interesting read" but continue feeding what you have always fed your dog; or
b) Rush out immediately and buy all the ingredients you need to start the 30 day WHOLEify challenge. (I've made this easy for you – you can download and print everything you need to do the challenge by visiting my website **www.WHOLEify.com/30-Day-Dog**); or
c) Decide you'd like to speak to me personally about your sick dog in which case I'd be happy to do a 90-minute iridology diagnostic and prescriptive phone consult with you (please visit my website **www.WHOLEify.com** to book your consult)

Whichever option you choose, I thank you for taking the time to read my book. I sincerely appreciate your interest in my work and my team and I would love to hear about your dog's progress as you #WHOLEifyMyDog (please send us updates to **hello@wholeify.com**)

Wishing you and your beautiful four-legged lots of fun, great health and a long happy life together.

"THE AVERAGE DOG IS A NICER PERSON THAN THE AVERAGE PERSON."

— Andy Rooney

CLIENT STORIES
(In their human's words)

To read more testimonials and see before and after photos please visit www.WHOLEify.com

Full Recovery from Heartworm, Skin Allergies and Hotspots, Seizures and Hypothryoidism

Lisa St. John from WHOLEify has been a blessing to both my husband and me and our Golden Retrievers Codey and Kaleb. We went to Lisa with two dogs that we were told by our vet, had incurable and deathly diseases. Codey had been tested and came out positive for heartworm (two tests both showed positive). We did not want to put our guy through what Western medicine calls the treatment for heartworm which is comparable to chemotherapy for humans and can quite often change the personality of your dog. Codey also has severe allergies that cause ear problems and large hotspots all over his body. Kaleb had been tested and diagnosed with Hypothyroidism, he would have seizures (one very bad grand mal), his hair was turning grey and got very curly. Again the vet said no cure and wanted to 'out' him on drugs. Lisa put them both on a WHOLEify Custom Wellness Plan. Codey's hot spots have disappeared, his ears have cleaned up for the first time in his life (9 years) and the vet was astounded that when he was tested for heartworm he was NEGATIVE! Kaleb's seizures have stopped, his hair has got darker and straightened out. The vet again was dumbstruck when Kaleb tested negative for hypothyroidism. In both cases the vet said that he had never seen anything like it ever before. His current diagnosis is this, "These are two of the healthiest dogs I have ever seen. I don't know what you are doing but it works so keep it up!"

Whether your best friends are sick or healthy, I truly and totally recommend WHOLEIfy and Lisa St. John and her wealth of information. Now with Lisa's help, our dogs are living long and happy lives.

Lonnie and Lynn L.
Washington, IL

Full Recovery from Tumors

My 9 year old Doberman had 8 tumors appear all over her body. After 2 months on the WHOLEify Program and their custom herbal formulas, they are dissolving at an amazing rate! I also feed it to my 10 year old Schitzu and 5 year old Daschund. This is a great program for ANY dog! They feel better, look better, and even smell better.

Client 86410 (name withheld by request)

Recovery from Thyroid Issue

I bought this formula from WHOLEify for my Doberman that has had a thyroid issue. He has been on this formula for several months and I was able to take him off his thyroid medication. Between his WHOLEify diet and the herbs, he has done really well and is thriving. It's been seven months now and I see a big difference.

Nancy H.

Health and Happiness Restored

The custom herbs from WHOLEify helped my dog tremendously! He was terribly sick and after starting a regime with these herbs, his heath improved so much he started acting like a puppy again! My dogs are thriving on the WHOLEify Wellness Program!

Client 76979 (name withheld by request)

No More Itchy Spots

My dog is 3 years old and has had itchy skin and some hot spots. I have tried everything including shampoos and some steroids. I changed her diet and started her on the immune enhancer from WHOLEify. So far so good. She isn't scratching and the spots have been healing nicely. I'm just sorry I haven't tried it sooner.

Client 85775 (name withheld by request)

Full Recovery From Bone Cancer

Mitch was scheduled to have his right rear leg removed as a result of bone cancer. I contacted Lisa St. John from WHOLeify and did everything she told me to do. We had him on all raw food, fruit, nuts, veggies, meat and herbs. It is now April of 2015. Mitch is now cancer free and is enjoying life on all 4 legs. Lisa has helped Mitch and our family through a very difficult time and was there by our side the entire time. I can never thank you enough for all you have done for us.

Andrea D. New York

Magic's Arthritis

Magic runs up and down the stairs now and no more hot spots! Been feeding him all natural foods - no processed dog food. All raw, whole foods. He is getting your Immune Enhancer and Joint Support and is doing great! He loves avocados, bananas and nuts!! Oh and he loves the almond milk. I also make him a smoothie in the morning. His coat is getting healthier as well. I cannot thank you enough for everything.

Casandra G. Pebble Beach, Ca.

Full Recovery From Cancerous Tumors

Brenna's story is an amazing story of love and dedication. Cassie McQuade from "Rescues by Cassie" in association with Hartmans Haven Dog Rescue and Catawba County Animal Control, rescued Brenna. Brenna had cancerous tumors throughout her body and a very large one on her leg. She was also pregnant, which came to the surprise of Cassie and the veterinarian. Brenna knew she was home when she met Cassie's daughter, Addison. It was Addison's love that gave Brenna the will to live and Cassie's amazing dedication, faith and love for animals, that provided Brenna with the care she needed to recover. Cassie contacted Lisa St. John when the tumors on Brenna's legs began to return and others began to appear despite the prior surgery to remove them.

Brenna was put on a natural diet to 'alkaline' her system and WHOLEify's custom herb program to support the natural healing and recovery process. Brenna is recovering beautifully and full of life. The tumors are vanishing and her body is becoming healthier and stronger every day.

Full Recovery From Lymphoma Cancer

My Dog, Ritz, 4 years old, was diagnosed with Lymphoma Cancer. My vet recommended euthanasia because the cancer was aggressive and had advanced. I heard of Lisa St. John from a few people at the dog beach where Fritz and I like to spend our afternoons. It was the best call I ever made. Lisa's approach to helping animals recover is logical and effective. I changed Ritz's diet by placing him on the recommended "natural diet " and herbal regime Lisa prescribed for him. By the end of September 2015, Ritz made a full recovery to the shock and amazement of my veterinarian, who could do nothing to help him and recommended he be put down. I will be forever grateful to Lisa and her vast knowledge of true health and healing. If you want healthy animals you have come to the right place.

A very happy client,

Donna M. Monterey, California

Client Stories

Full Recovery From Lymphoma Cancer

I have 4 year old Doberman named Diva. Diva was diagnosed with Lymphoma Cancer 6 months ago. I heard of Lisa St. John through a lady I met at the dog park. I called Lisa as soon as we returned home. I did everything Lisa told me to do. I changed Diva over to Lisa's prescribed diet therapy plan and herbs. The vets were not happy with my decision to go the natural route to help Diva but it felt right to me especially after talking with Lisa. Lisa was so patient with me and was there for us every step of the way. Her detoxification and alkaline diet plan works. My Diva is now Cancer free! If you have a sick pet you need to contact WHOLEify right away. Thank you Lisa!

    Rita J.

Full Recovery From Epilepsy

Nero, our beloved 7 year old Shepherd cross was suffering from epilepsy and having violent seizures on average three times a week. Lisa St. John from WHOLEify put him on a custom herb formulation and gave him a brand new diet. He had one seizure a week after starting the program but has not had a single seizure since.

    Our vet cannot believe it. He is healthy and happy to this day and is no longer diagnosed with epilepsy.

    Patty G.

Full Recovery From Arthritis

Sadie is our 13 year old Australian Shepherd. She is a cherished, family member and loyal friend. Recently Sadie began treatment for severe arthritis of the spine after we began to notice increasing difficulty for her to get around comfortably. Treatment was in early April of 2004 and consisted of 3 laser acupressure sessions spaced at one week intervals. Our vet also prescribed a non-steroid anti-inflammatory.

    After her second treatment, Sadie developed a fever and refused to eat. Lab tests were ordered on the day of her third treatment and according to our vet, Sadie's white blood cell count was very high. An infection was indicated, possibly pancreatic. Ultrasound later found that her spleen was enlarged. Exploratory surgery was recommended. My basic instinct told me to wait.

At Sadie's age and in her weakened condition, I worried about the added stress on her body. The vet assured me that Sadie could live without a spleen but if the mass which was growing inside her was cancerous, it could spread to her liver and become terminal. I became anxious and fearful that Sadie might not survive surgery or be with us much longer. She would not eat or play. She looked as though she was just too tired and wanted to give up. I then resorted to faithful prayer and guidance from God.

My answer soon came in the form of Lisa St. John from WHOLEify… We noticed an instant improvement after starting with WHOLEify …each day Sadie's energy slowly increased and her appetite returned. She was starting to heal and quickly! She actually began playing with her toys again and looked forward to our walks. With each passing day she has continued to improve. It is so good to have a holistic alternative to conventional treatments for animals. We are honored and grateful for Lisa.

Rosannn L, Monterey, CA

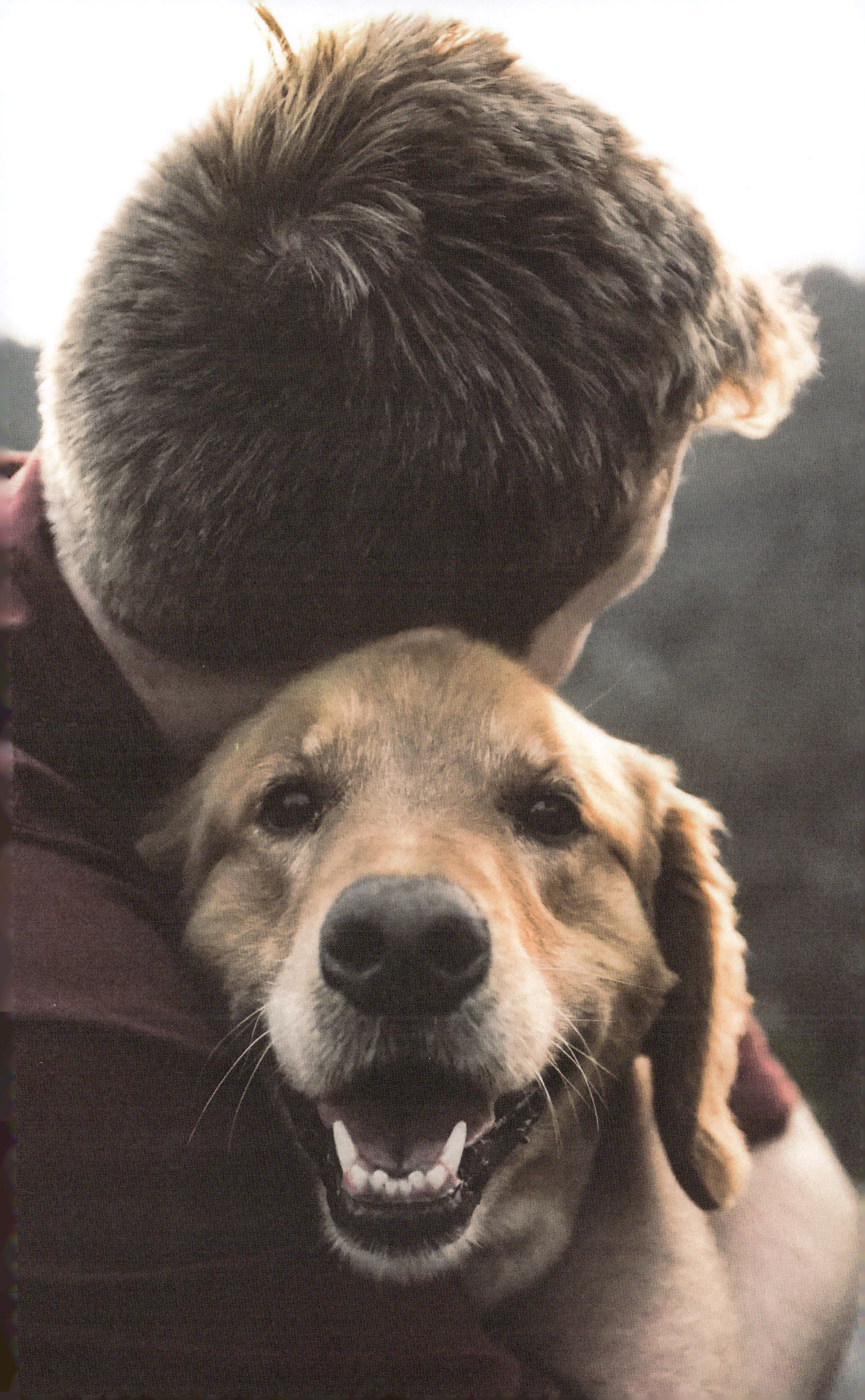

"DOGS ARE OUR LINK TO PARADISE. THEY DON'T KNOW EVIL... OR JEALOUSY... OR DISCONTENT. TO SIT WITH A DOG ON A HILLSIDE ON A GLORIOUS AFTERNOON IS TO BE BACK IN EDEN, WHERE DOING NOTHING WAS NOT BORING... ... IT WAS PEACE."

— Milan Kundera

TAKE THE #WHOLEify 30 DAY CHALLENGE

If you are on the fence about whether or not to try feeding your dog the WHOLEify way, doing my 30 day challenge is a great way for you to take it for a test run. If you follow my instructions **I absolutely guarantee you will notice a visible difference in your dog within 7 days**. And after 30 dogs your dog will be like a brand new dog in terms of energy levels, movement, and even muscle tone. Now please remember that Rome wasn't built in a day so you can't expect your dog to totally transform their health in 30 days. It took them many years to reach their current state, so re-building their health takes time too, however by taking up my 30 day challenge I guarantee you will notice such a change in your dog that you will never look back. And if you're skeptical – good! What's the worst that can happen? You don't notice a major difference and prefer to go back to the old way of feeding. What have you lost by trying it – nothing! But your dog has EVERYTHING to gain.

Alright, ready to get started? One word of caution. Please do not "half-arse" this (apologies for the expression but I learned it downunder and think it's brilliant). Meaning please don't do this challenge half way and mix in your old food. Either you transition completely to the new food as outlined below – or not at all.

You will want to begin by removing all processed pet foods.

Start your dog off with cooked foods to transition. I like to start them on chicken soup. Homemade soup not store bought, frozen or canned.

Chicken Soup

Ingredients:
- Chicken thighs
- Carrots
- Ginger root

Place in a large pot of water and cook for 1 hour
If you do not like to cook then purchase your dog a roasted chicken from the grocery store and start him out on that.

Day 1- 7

Breakfast and Dinner options

1. Soup
2. Roasted chicken with raw carrots or any raw veggie

Snack

Fruit, trail mix, veggies…

Day 7-9

Reduce amount of soup or chicken and in another bowl place a handful of raw ground meat

Day 9-30

Transition completely to raw fresh food
Follow the diet shown on Chapter 6
Feed your dog - Raw meat, raw veggies, fruit, nuts and seeds.

Note: *Never feed your dog frozen veggies or fruits – only feed in season fresh produce.*

If your dog is showing signs of detox such as runny eyes, flu like symptoms etc. I strongly recommend ordering the Immune Enhancer to support their system – visit **www.Wholeify.com** and use promo code HeartMyDog for 15% off.

Please take a photo of your dog from all angles – front, both sides and a view of them sitting from behind. In 30 days please take new photos and compare them! Please email them to us we would love to see your dog's progress. Please send to hello@wholeify.com

"EVERYTHING I KNOW, I LEARNED FROM DOGS."

- Nora Roberts

WHOLEify

WHOLISTIC WELLNESS FOR HORSES & DOGS

www.Wholeify.com

Save 15% On Any WHOLEify Product
Visit www.WHOLEify.com
USE PROMOCODE HeartMyDog

Save 15%
Promo Code
HeartMyDog

WHOLEify Immune Enhancer™
WHOLEify Puppy Formula™
WHOLEify K9 Complete™
WHOLEify K9 Senior™
WHOLEify Joint Support™

"IT ALL STARTED WHEN MY DOG BEGAN GETTING FREE ROLL OVER MINUTES."

– Jay London

ABOUT LISA ST. JOHN

Lisa St. John is a Wholistic Naturopath specializing in Equine and Canine health and wellness for over twenty years. When she was 38 years old she was diagnosed with a stage 4 brain tumor on the pituitary gland. She was told she was beyond conventional treatment and given two months to live.

By chance, Lisa met Howard Straus, the grandson of Dr. Max Gerson who created the Gerson Therapy for advanced degenerative diseases.

Howard's dog had a tumor and he was looking for natural alternatives to help treat his dog. While working with his dog, Lisa started researching the Gerson Therapy and quickly switched her diet to eat only raw foods and juices. But there was still a missing piece of the puzzle. She continued her research and discovered Dr. Morse, a Florida-based Naturopath who used herbs to accelerate the body's cellular regeneration rate. It changed Lisa's life and gave her a deeper understanding of the herbal protocols used in her **Wholeify Wellness Programs**™ to transform the health of horses and dogs for over twenty years.

Lisa's clients span the globe - from top level performance and Olympic horses to beloved backyard trail horses; from polo ponies, dressage horses, eventers, race horses and hunter jumpers to fox hunters, reiners, cutting horses, barrel racers, endurance horses and vaulters. Lisa's clients include horses owned by members of the royal family, celebrities and regular people searching for a natural alternative to conventional medicine.

In the dog world, Lisa has worked with over a hundred different breeds of dogs, from champion show-dogs to lap-dogs and all the "four-legged fur children" in between - including senior dogs with special needs, puppies and females used for breeding.

Lisa St. John has been featured in a wide range of national and international media including articles in the Sun Post News, the Daily Herald, The Horse Gazette, Ojai Valley News, The Courier News, The Herald - Monterey, and Holistic Horseman. She has been host of two west coast radio shows - the

Animal Talk and Talking With The Animals and a midwest based radio show, Animal Zone. WHOLEify Your Dog is Lisa's first book in a series of three books on equine and canine health.

Lisa can be contacted via her website **www.WHOLEify.com**

"YOU CAN SAY ANY FOOLISH THING TO A DOG, AND THE DOG WILL GIVE YOU A LOOK THAT SAYS, 'WOW, YOU'RE RIGHT! I NEVER WOULD'VE THOUGHT OF THAT!'"

— Dave Barry

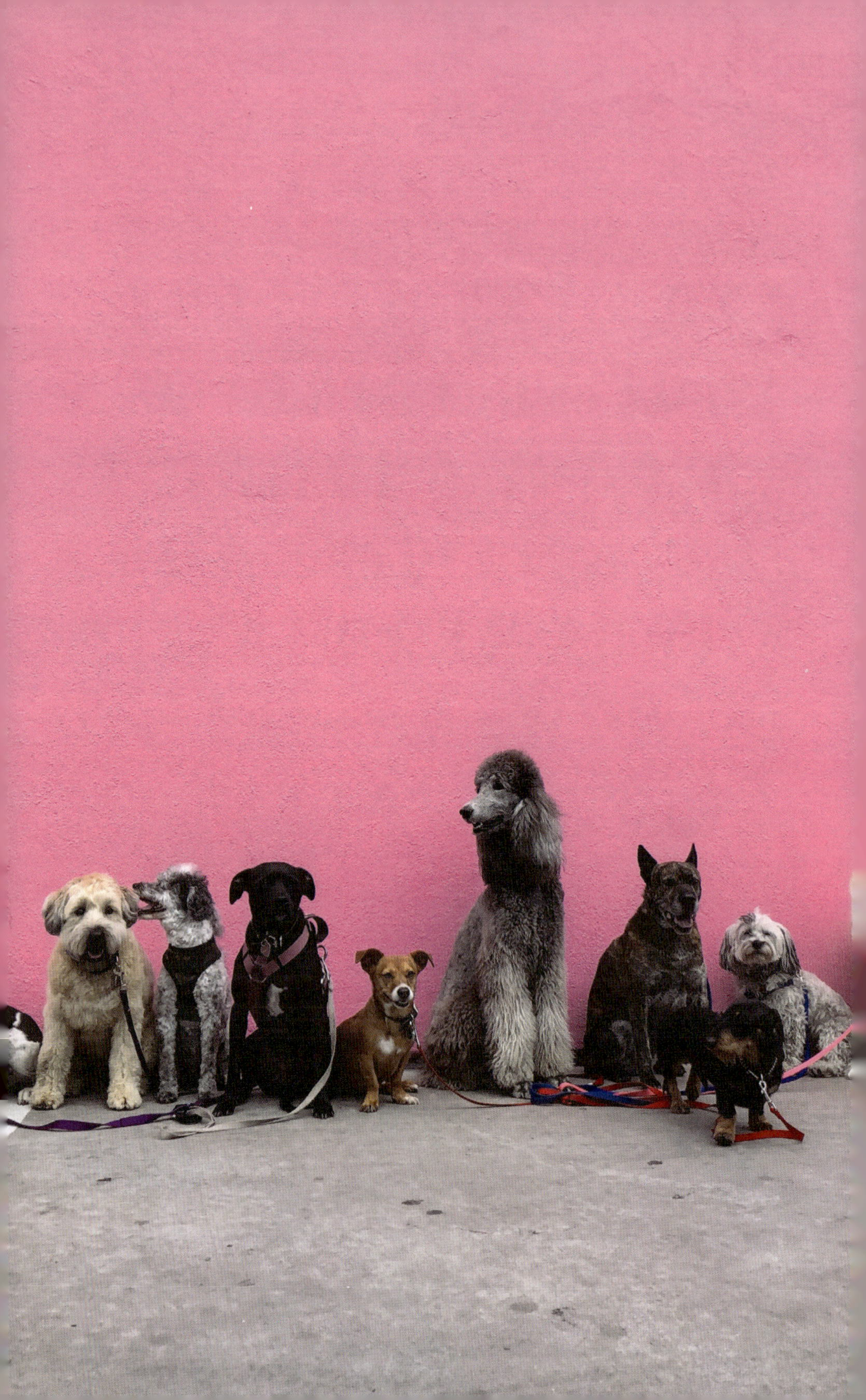

REFERENCES

George Perry of Pennsylvania state University - Expert in ancient DNA

Dr. Malgorzata Pilot - School of Life Science at University of Lincoln

Bridgett Von Holt - Princeton University

Science News

Dr. Robert Morse ND. , D.S.c , M.H - Author of the Detox Source book

Dr. Ian Billinghurst - Veterinarian in Australia - Author of Give Your Dog a Bone.

Animal Cancer Society

American Institute for Cancer Research

Dr. Thomas N. Seyfried PhD

Dr. Stanislaw Burzynski, MD, PhD

Dr. Joseph Mercola, DO

Dr. Gaston Cornu-Labat M.D

Dr. Nicholas Gonzalez MD

Dr. Galina Migalko MD, NMD

Dr. Manuela Malaguti-Boyle PhD, ND

Dr. Matthias Rath, MD

Dr. Veronique Desaulniers, DC, BVS

Dr. Rick Palmquist DVM

Dr. Elizabeth Pantzer DVM

Dr. Robert J Silver DVM, MS

Dr. Gary Richter, DVM, MS

Dr. Allen Schoen, DVM, MS

Dr. Marlene Siegel, DVM

Dr. Martin Goldstein, DVM

Dr. Jean Dodds, DVM

Dr. Judy Morgan, DVM

Dr. PJ Broadfoot, DVM

1. A. Prahl DVM, L. Guptill DVM, PhD, Dipl ACVIM, N. W. Glickman MS, MPH, PhD, M. Tetrick DVM, PhD, and L. T. Glickman VMD, DrPH, "Time Trends and Risk Factors for Diabetes Mellitus in Cats Presented to Veterinary Teaching Hospitals," *Journal of Feline Medicine and Surgery* 9, no. 5, October 2007, 351-358.
2. Justine S. Patrick, "Deconstructing the Regulatory Façade: Why Confused Consumers Feed their Pets Ring Dings and Krispy Kremes," Digital Access to Scholarship at Harvard (DASH), April 2006.
3. Patrick, "Deconstructing."
4. Patrick, "Deconstructing."
5. Christopher S. Cowell, Neil P. Stout, Mark F. Brinkman, Edward A. Moser, and Stephen W. Crane, "History of Pet Food Manufacture in the United States," *Small Animal Clinical Nutrition*, 4th ed. Walsworth Publishing Company, 2000, 129.
6. Cowell and others, 129.
7. Cowell and others, 132-134.
8. Justine S. Patrick, "Deconstructing the Regulatory Façade: Why Confused Consumers Feed their Pets Ring Dings and Krispy Kremes," Digital Access to Scholarship at Harvard (DASH), April 2006.
9. "Hill's Pet Nutrition, Inc.," Funding Universe. *International Directory of Company Histories* 27, St. James Press, 1999.
10. Justine S. Patrick, "Deconstructing the Regulatory Façade: Why Confused Consumers Feed their Pets Ring Dings and Krispy Kremes," Digital Access to Scholarship at Harvard (DASH), April 2006.
11. Patrick, "Deconstructing."
12. The Raw Food Diet For Dogs by Anahad O'Connor – New York Times

Printed in Great Britain
by Amazon